LEADING IMPROVEMENT FOR
GIFTED AND TALENTED STUDENTS

JOHN MUNRO

Published in 2025 by Amba Press, Melbourne, Australia
www.ambapress.com.au

First published in 2024 by ACER Press, an imprint of
Australian Council for Educational Research Ltd

© John Munro 2025

This book is copyright. All rights reserved. Except under the conditions described in the *Copyright Act 1968* of Australia and subsequent amendments, and any exceptions permitted under the current statutory licence scheme administered by Copyright Agency (www.copyright.com.au), no part of this publication may be reproduced, stored in a retrieval system, transmitted, broadcast or communicated in any form or by any means, optical, digital, electronic, mechanical, photocopying, recording or otherwise, without the written permission of the publisher.

Edited by Shaneen Goodwin
Cover design, text design and typesetting by Nada Backovic
Cover image © Depiction Images/Shutterstock.com

Paperback ISBN 9781923569102
ePub ISBN 9781923569119

A catalogue record for this book is available from the National Library of Australia.

FOREWORD

> *Research is revealing the powerful impact that school leadership teams can have in improving the quality of teaching and learning. Effective leaders create cultures of high expectations, provide clarity about what teachers are to teach and students are to learn, establish strong professional learning communities and lead ongoing efforts to improve teaching practices. (Masters 2012)*

School leadership is an increasingly complex, highly demanding role. School leaders are accountable for a broad range of factors and outcomes and to a wide array of stakeholders. In establishing short- and long-term goals for improving outcomes for students, school leaders must turn their minds not only to performance indicators and targets but to the methods, approaches and strategies through which those targets can be achieved.

Research tells us that schools and school systems that embrace evidence-based practice models are those most likely to achieve their goals of improving outcomes for young people. It also tells us that it is school leaders who play a critical role in identifying, implementing, embedding and leading evidence-based practice.

The 'High impact strategies for school leaders' series is designed as a resource for those busy school leaders whose ultimate aim is to improve outcomes for all learners. Each book in the series, focusing on a different domain within the school environment, unpacks for school leaders the ways high-impact strategies and practices can be applied to achieve improvement goals. Written by highly regarded experts in their fields, the series seeks to focus attention on the role of school leaders in driving the processes that result in effective school and classroom practice and improved outcomes for students and help them navigate through the dizzying array of information about 'what works' and what doesn't.

In *Leading improvement for gifted and talented students*, Associate Professor John Munro highlights the role of principals and other school-based leaders in leading improvement in provision for gifted and talented students across domains. Munro presents a range of evidenced-informed practices that can be used as a focus for teacher professional learning and school improvement.

Through his work with the University of Melbourne as well as state, national and international associations for gifted education, John Munro has a wealth of experience and knowledge in the strategies and practices that lead to long-lasting and impactful change in supporting gifted and talented students to achieve their potential. *Leading improvement for gifted and talented students* provides research evidence and practical tools to support key practices in schools, including identifying high-ability and high-level outcomes, supporting twice-exceptional students, students from diverse backgrounds, differentiation, classroom culture and social and emotional wellbeing. In addition, an introductory chapter unpacks the importance of assessing the current situation in individual school contexts before embarking on actions for improvement.

Munro draws on some of his own well-received research and the work of other educational authorities in constructing the high-impact practices that shape this book. Together, these provide an effective framework for schools and school leaders to strengthen their provision for all gifted and talented students in their care.

CONTENTS

Foreword		iii
Chapter 1:	Improved provision for high-ability and gifted students	1
Chapter 2:	What are high-level outcomes?	17
Chapter 3:	How do students achieve high-level outcomes?	27
Chapter 4:	What do multiple high-ability and gifted learning profiles look like?	41
Chapter 5:	Twice-exceptional students	53
Chapter 6:	How to identify students who display high-level outcomes	73
Chapter 7:	Does a student have a high-ability and gifted learning profile?	95
Chapter 8:	How to differentiate the regular curriculum	125
Chapter 9:	How to differentiate regular classroom teaching to foster high-level outcomes	155
Chapter 10:	How to differentiate classroom culture and climate to achieve high-level outcomes	173
Chapter 11:	High-ability and gifted students and social–emotional issues	185
Chapter 12:	Learning from high-ability and gifted students	199
Chapter 13:	Implementing improved provision for high-ability and gifted students: a whole-school approach	211
Chapter 14:	Where to in future for high-ability and gifted provision?	233

CHAPTER 1

Improved provision for high-ability and gifted students

Introduction

This book is about how a school's leadership team can guide and lead a school to enhance its capacity to optimise the learning outcomes of high-ability and gifted students.

Education providers around the world are showing an increased interest in catering for high-ability and gifted students. There is also a growing interest internationally in the factors that enhance talent development and the achievement of excellent outcomes. In Australia, a recurring outcome from international assessment comparisons such as PISA is that Australian students in the highest ability bands underachieve and are not achieving at their expected levels.

The extent to which these students fail to realise their learning capacity and achieve high-level or talented outcomes has been reported by federal and state inquiries into educational provision for them. The inquiry of the Australian Senate Select Committee for the Education of Gifted and Talented Children reported that between 38 and 75 per cent of gifted students achieve below their capability level and between

15 and 40 per cent leave school before completing year 12 (Senate Select Committee 2001:14). A later inquiry in Victoria (Education and Training Committee 2012) reported that up to 50 per cent of all gifted school students achieve below their capability level.

This represents a loss at the individual and societal levels, at a time when knowledge enhancement, talent and innovation are seen as important for the future. A key issue for school leaders here is how to optimise the high-ability and gifted learning capital in their schools, so that all students achieve their potential.

Australia is addressing this in various ways. Victoria, for example, has established the Centre for Higher Education Studies (CHES), a state-wide centre of excellence that will focus on the learning needs of high-achieving senior secondary school–aged students. In 2019 New South Wales introduced a policy to identify and extend gifted students in all public schools (NSW Government Education 2022). This policy includes a High Potential and Gifted Education (HPGE) Advisory Group. It notes that there is much to do to improve provision for these students and, in particular, to equip teachers and schools to provide for them. Other states and countries are making similar provisions.

School leaders also acknowledge the need to enhance the professional knowledge and capacity of schools to realise their goals in this area. Craig Petersen, the head of the NSW Secondary Principals' Council, noted the need for 'support and expertise' for the policy to be achieved (Baker 26 November 2021).

For schools to change their educational provision, they need to modify their pedagogic practice. This requires the school to develop a professional knowledge among the teaching staff that will scaffold the change. This includes staff learning to implement teaching practices that will improve provision for high-ability and gifted learners, and having the motivation, confidence and commitment to achieve this goal.

The main ideas in this chapter are shown in Figure 1.1.

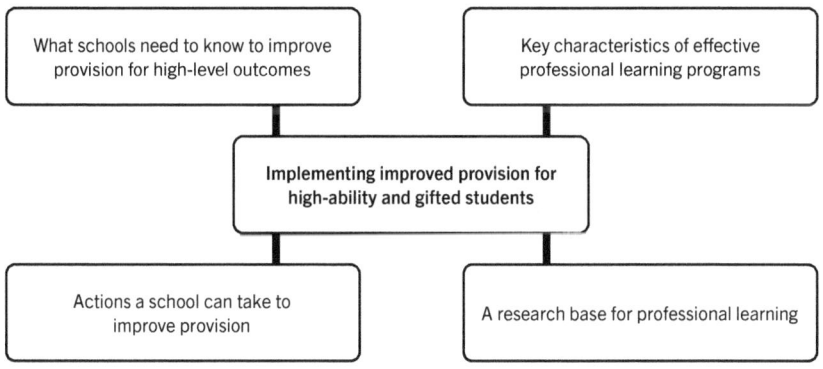

Figure 1.1. Toward improved provision for high-ability and gifted students

What do schools need to know?

Improved provision requires enhanced professional knowledge. This is achieved through professional learning. The school leadership team leads and scaffolds this learning. Aspects of professional knowledge identified in this book include:

> ❯ what high-level and talented outcomes look like and how they differ from the outcomes of 'regular-ability' students (see Chapter 2)
>
> ❯ the ways of learning that lead to the high-level outcomes (see Chapter 3)
>
> ❯ the learning profiles that can lead to high-level outcomes (see Chapters 4 and 5)
>
> ❯ how to identify the students in a cohort who can potentially achieve high-level or talented outcomes (see Chapters 6 and 7)
>
> ❯ how to plan and implement educational provision that optimises high-level and talented outcomes (see Chapters 8, 9 and 10)

> how to take account of the emotional and social characteristics of high-ability and gifted learners (see Chapter 11)

> learning from high-ability and gifted students (see Chapter 12)

> implementing a whole-school approach to improved provision (see Chapter 13)

> where to in future for high-ability and gifted provision (see Chapter 14).

Equipped with this knowledge, teachers are more able to hone their teaching and plan it in a way that scaffolds and fosters how high-ability and gifted students learn. They can also target their teaching towards different learning profiles, some of which are often neglected or ignored in provision for high-ability and gifted students. They are also more likely to effectively identify students who can achieve high-level outcomes (many schools use procedures that identify only a limited subset of high-ability and gifted students). Teachers can optimise high-level outcomes by differentiating teaching, modifying the curriculum and implementing appropriate classroom climate and cultures.

The sequence of professional knowledge areas can also contribute to a school-wide professional learning action plan.

Characteristics of effective professional learning programs in gifted education

The *Global principles for professional learning in gifted education* published by the World Council for Gifted and Talented Children (WCGTC) (2021) provide school leadership teams with a framework that can guide the development and implementation of professional learning programs. It recommends that these programs should:

1. be differentiated or 'tiered' to match different teaching responsibilities and equip all educators to teach gifted children
2. reflect best practice and evidence-based research relating to gifted education provision
3. focus on how the student 'as a whole' operates and learns
4. have the breadth necessary to cover multiple forms and levels of giftedness, multiple identification protocols, a range of programs, and options for modifying curriculum and instruction
5. recognise and value equitably the learning profiles of the range of students in classrooms
6. be appropriate for the range of professionals likely to work with gifted students; this includes administrators, counsellors, psychologists and special educators
7. present gifted education as an integral part of the whole school program and provision
8. provide ongoing professional learning opportunities for teachers to extend their knowledge and skills
9. be included in educational policy at the relevant jurisdictional levels (regional, state, federal) with appropriate accountability and monitoring protocols and collaboration between all stakeholders
10. equip or empower educators to be effective advocates for and supporters of gifted students and their access to optimal learning opportunities.

These principles provide school leaders with a valuable set of criteria for designing and evaluating the professional learning opportunities provided for staff.

Actions for an improved provision agenda

This book describes the professional knowledge a school needs to enhance its provision for high-ability and gifted students. While it recommends actions school leaders can take, it is more than a 'toolbox'. It applies the principles identified by the WCGTC and elaborates many of the procedures in the Australian Association for the Education of the Gifted and Talented (AAEGT) (2022) *Gifted policy*. It also provides a road map and systematic approach to guide and inform leaders' decision-making in relation to achieving improved provision.

To plan an agenda for improving its provision for high-ability and gifted students, a school can:

> identify its current existing knowledge and practice

> identify what its improved outcomes would 'look like', that is, what it would achieve when it provides for these students

> identify what additional professional knowledge it needs to reposition its provision

> plan a professional learning trajectory to reposition it from its current position to the desired position.

This agenda is shown pictorially in Figure 1.2.

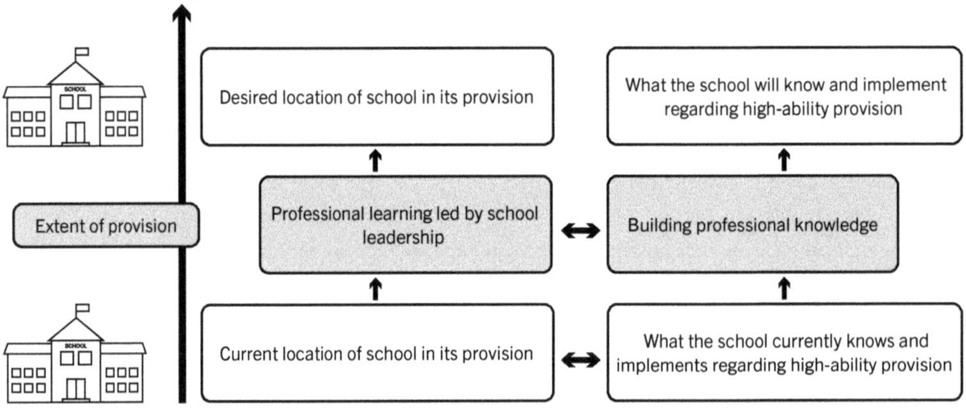

Figure 1.2. The interacting pathways for improving provision for high-ability and gifted students

These 2 channels are linked. A change in a school's provision requires a corresponding development in its professional knowledge. To this end, each chapter includes a 'What your school can do now' section. This section describes actions school leaders might take to target issues discussed in the chapter. Cumulatively, they provide a professional learning program for the agenda.

Professional knowledge needs a research base

The findings related to high-level learning outcomes and the recommendations made in this book are, as much as possible, based on contemporary research. As well as using the results of individual studies, this book draws on research that investigates the combined outcomes of several studies on a particular aspect. These are 'meta-analyses' (Cooper and Hedges 2009). They synthesise the findings from individual studies, report similarities and differences and sometimes explain why differences arise. They are useful for the study of high ability and giftedness, particularly because some individual studies have few participants and apply to specific age or cultural groups.

You are probably aware that the high-ability category includes students who are described as gifted or talented. However, the terms 'high ability', 'gifted' and 'talented' have been defined in several ways and are used inconsistently, which can affect how research is interpreted. Some studies also report contradictory or conflicting results. Reference is made to relevant research in each of the topics examined. It will be used to support the recommendations made.

The content of this book is intended to enhance middle leaders' professional knowledge, as well as that of the leadership team. Throughout the chapters, reference is made to additional relevant sources of information that middle leaders may decide to pursue.

What your school can do now

The decision to target improved provision will probably be made by the school leadership team. The early steps include making various school-wide decisions, such as the goals of the enhanced provision and the policy that will guide it, the personnel who will lead the improvement agenda, why current provision is insufficient and how the professional knowledge of the school will be developed to underpin progress in changed practice.

The remaining sections in this chapter present areas of activity through which the leadership team can initiate action towards improved provision in gifted education. The focus at this point is on your leadership team being aware that it may need to act in each area and to take the first steps. It is not expected that you will end up with the 'final outcome'. Instead, it is likely that each area of activity will be modified as your school works collaboratively through Chapters 2 to 14 and builds a school-wide professional knowledge.

Develop a vision

Schools can develop both a broad vision and a goal or ambition for the provision of gifted education. This can involve the team collaboratively unpacking their vision of what their school will 'look like' when the improved provision is in place. Members can do this by responding to a guiding set of questions, such as:

> How will the school curriculum look different?
> What will the school be 'known for' in terms of high-ability and gifted provision?
> What will its high-ability and gifted students be learning differently? What will they be saying about the school?
> What will teachers be doing differently?

In parallel with developing the vision, the school leadership can specify its long-term general goal for the provision. Schools typically have the goal of providing the opportunity for all students to achieve optimal learning and development. The goal for high-ability and gifted provision could elaborate this in a follow-up sentence that specifies what this might look like for this cohort in the particular context of the school.

Plan how the provision will be led

The school leadership team will probably not have the time to take a 'hands-on' role in leading the provision. The team can convene a group of school staff who can be equipped to act as middle leaders or coaches of high-ability and gifted education provision. It may also be appropriate that the leadership appoint one or more staff to lead this group and oversee implementation; they will be the coordinators or leaders of high-ability and gifted provision.

Teachers who have completed advanced studies in gifted and talented education, such as postgraduate education or extensive professional development, would usually qualify as coaches. Where teachers with specialised skills or qualifications are not available, a school can provide professional learning for a group of teachers who show an interest and motivation in provision for these students.

These personnel can practically lead the improved provision. They work at 'the interface' between leadership and teaching staff by collecting information that informs decision-making by leadership along with school and teaching practices. They also provide instructional leadership to foster staff thinking, dialogue and research about high-ability and gifted learning and teaching at the whole-school level. This includes clarifying explicit expectations regarding student learning and teaching and engaging in mentoring and coaching.

Evaluate current provision

A school's middle leaders can ascertain and evaluate current overall provision and practice and communicate this to the school leadership team. To do this, they can use resources such as this book to develop tools that evaluate school procedures, programs, and practices for high-ability and gifted students and indicate where, when and how their learning profiles and achievement are targeted. They can also identify and collate the resources currently available for use in this provision.

Begin an action plan

Starting an action plan can involve identifying key areas of early activity, such as those discussed in this section. It can also include specifying:

> who will be involved in the implementation, how this will be negotiated, how teachers and faculties in the school will be familiarised with the intended agenda and why it is appropriate

> the possible time frame for implementation

> an estimate of the resources needed

> how the voices of students, teachers and the wider school community will be included

> how the innovation aligns with other school priorities, possible risks for the school in undertaking it and how these risks might be managed

> initial indicators for monitoring the progress or success of the innovation

> how the outcomes of the implementation will be assessed.

Understand jurisdictional policies

Most educational systems have policies relating to high-ability and gifted provision and some mandate provision (for example, the HPGE policy for all NSW public schools). It is recommended that a school be familiar with the expectations and requirements of its educational jurisdiction. The leadership team can evaluate their current provision in terms of these policies, again with input from the middle leaders, and use the systemic policies to direct future provision.

They can also identify and ascertain the relevant support services offered by their educational system and other external bodies, such as the professional associations that advocate for gifted and talented students. Some systems provide professional development programs, such as the HPGE orientation program offered via the NSW Department of Education (2022).

Investigate and collaborate

Schools can benefit from researching how other schools and educational institutions in their community make provision for gifted and talented students. This may also open up opportunities for future collaboration. School and/or middle leaders can investigate how neighbouring schools currently make high-ability and gifted provision and whether they would be interested in collaborations relating to:

> shared professional development for staff

> advanced learning opportunities for students, such as access to specialist subjects or programs, extra-curricular activities, and collaborative learning activities such as research investigations and problem-solving

> shared resources and learning facilities

> transition and early entry opportunities for students between early childhood, primary, secondary, and tertiary education facilities.

These opportunities can initially be pursued through leadership and school community networks.

Some of these collaborations can be administered using virtual classroom or video conferencing technology. They are particularly important for schools with smaller enrolments, those that are in more remote locations and those that educate socioeconomically disadvantaged cohorts.

School and/or middle leaders can also look into additional sources of advanced learning in their communities. They can investigate possible collaborations with local tertiary institutions (universities and TAFE colleges), research institutions or organisations in domains such as history, music, visual or performing arts, sport, science, technology and engineering, and information services and libraries run by local and state government or universities. They can also pursue collaborations with the providers of online learning courses or virtual classrooms.

Consult the broader community

Schools can also optimise the success of their improvement agendas by planning a strategy for collaborating with families, parents and carers and other stakeholders in the school and broader communities. This includes ways of hearing and responding to the voices of the students involved.

Parents' and carers' perceptions of their high-ability and gifted children, their past learning experiences and the issues and challenges they face frequently differ from those of their children's educators. Earlier expectations may not have been realised. Some may have not been aware of the opportunities and pathways available. Their insights, and those of their children, can contribute to the improved provision.

The leadership and coaching teams can develop a plan for engaging positively and communicating constructively with parents and carers and the broader community and for capturing the student voice. The plan can include procedures for supporting parents and carers and for drawing on potential support from families and community groups.

Plan a professional learning program

Schools can help build the knowledge necessary to underpin the provision of gifted education by planning a staff professional learning program comprising 2 components:

> the relevant professional knowledge

> the strategic teaching that matches this knowledge.

In this book, professional knowledge is described in Chapters 2 to 14. It is recommended that staff work through this content collaboratively and negotiate an 'agreed' or 'shared' knowledge in groups led by the high-ability and gifted education coaches. The 'What your school can do now' sections of these chapters recommend strategic actions teachers can take. Teachers can trial these recommendations, monitor their success, modify them if necessary and share them with colleagues. The high-ability and gifted education coaches can lead this aspect by modelling teaching procedures and guiding staff to implement them in their teaching.

Summary

The set of activities that have been discussed here targets the first steps in implementing improved provision of gifted education and provides the initial 'infrastructure' for this. The following chapters elaborate aspects of the provision. It is likely that the outcomes of the activities in this chapter will be revisited and modified more than once, as the leadership and coaches learn more about this provision. It is also recommended that as the leadership and coaches lead their staff through the content, they regularly ask them to identify explicitly what they have learnt, both in terms of their understanding of high-ability and gifted learning and the teaching protocols that support it. Teaching staff can contribute to a school-wide emerging 'code of teaching practice' for high-ability and gifted provision.

Remember:

> Identify the professional knowledge your school needs to enhance its provision for high-ability and gifted students.

> Apply the characteristics of effective professional learning programs.

> Know the key actions to use.

The professional learning pathway unpacked explicitly in this book shows the way to enhanced provision for these students. This will assist schools to optimise the likelihood of high-ability and talented outcomes, enhance the life options of all students, and contribute to building the knowledge capital of the community and culture.

References

AAEGT (Australian Association for the Education of the Gifted and Talented) (2022) *Gifted policy*, AAEGT, accessed 12 September 2023. https://irp.cdn-website.com/2d95ae4a/files/uploaded/AAEGT%20Gifted%20Policy%202022.pdf

Baker J (26 November 2021) 'Fears gifted students will languish without help', *The Sydney Morning Herald*, accessed 11 July 2023. https://www.smh.com.au/national/nsw/fears-gifted-students-will-languish-without-help-20211125-p59c2c.html

Cooper H and Hedges LV (2009) 'Research synthesis as a scientific process', in Cooper H, Hedges LV and Valentine JC (eds) *The handbook of research synthesis and meta-analysis*, Russell Sage Foundation, New York.

Education and Training Committee (2012) *Inquiry into the education of gifted and talented students*, Parliament of Victoria.

NSW Department of Education (2022) *High potential and gifted education*, NSW Government Website – Education, NSW Government, accessed 13 September 2023. https://education.nsw.gov.au/policy-library/policies/pd-2004-0051

Senate Select Committee (2001) *The education of gifted and talented children*, Australian Government Publishing Service, Canberra, accessed 11 September 2023. http://pandora.nla.gov.au/pan/25300/20020605-0000/www.aph.gov.au/senate/committee/EET_CTTE/gifted/report/contents.htm

WCGTC (World Council for Gifted and Talented Children) (2021) *Global principles for professional learning in gifted education*, accessed 12 September 2023. https://world-gifted.org/professional-learning-global-principles.pdf

CHAPTER 2

What are high-level outcomes?

Introduction

High-level and talented outcomes are indicators of a high or gifted learning ability. To foster and promote these outcomes, educators and school leaders need to know what these outcomes actually 'look like' and how they differ from the outcomes of 'regular' learning students.

Any teaching information codes the knowledge and skills students are expected to learn. Students differ in how well they learn this knowledge and the outcomes they form.

The main ideas in this chapter are shown in Figure 2.1.

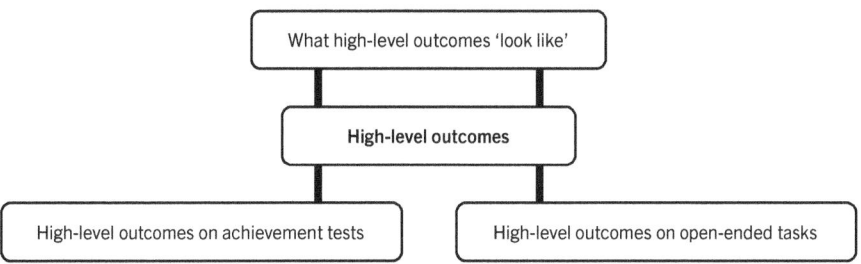

Figure 2.1. High-level outcomes and what they look like

What do high-level outcomes look like?

High-level and talented outcomes are shown as outstanding performance in the domains of all subjects across the board. They have also been described as 'advanced' or 'top of the range'. The qualities of talented outcomes are described as 'excellent', 'expert', 'masterly', 'original', 'creative', 'atypical' or 'unexpected'.

These outcomes are not random. They come from students interpreting the information presented by teachers more comprehensively. These interpretations may include:

> concepts and relationships that are not mentioned explicitly in the teaching information

> unexpected possibilities and novel ways of thinking about the ideas.

High-level outcomes show evidence of students spontaneously analysing and synthesising ideas, usually in novel, innovative ways.

We can conceptualise high-level outcomes using regular outcomes as a reference point. Regular students essentially learn at least part of what is given in the teaching. High-ability and gifted students end up knowing more than this. They show it in how they interpret the teaching, the additional ideas in their understanding and the questions and possibilities they raise.

The high-level outcomes of different students vary. Some show an understanding that extends or goes beyond the teaching but that is largely linked with it. Others show an understanding that goes further, and either questions part of the teaching or raises quite divergent possibilities. Some form an 'expert' interpretation; they can think about the topic from multiple perspectives at once, can see possible implications and possibilities and solve comparatively high-level problems and issues.

In other words, the high-level outcomes are not homogeneous. They vary in their complexity and sophistication. Even though they all substantially add to or modify the initial teaching information, we can think of them on a continuum, based on how much they differ from the teaching information.

Statistically, high-level outcomes are usually in the top 15 to 25 per cent of outcomes for the regular classroom cohort, although this range is arbitrary (Harding et al. 2018:5). Gagné (2020), for example, segments this range into a 'talented' section (the top 10 per cent of outcomes) and a 'high-achievement' section (the next 15 per cent of outcomes). For brevity, here this range is referred to overall as 'high-level' outcomes.

Students can display high-level outcomes in all domains (for example, English, mathematics, languages, science and technology, humanities, arts, social sciences, economics and business, sports and athletics) and at all levels of primary and secondary education.

Scenario

Charlie

Charlie, a year 1 student, showed an example when listening in class to the narrative *The 39-storey treehouse* by Andy Griffiths and Terry Denton. The text refers briefly to 'swivel chairs'. While listening, Charlie began to move. When asked to explain, Charlie described a dynamic impression of how these chairs might be propelled and 'steered' by a 'rider' using their body. Charlie also inferred how the authors may have got their ideas. Charlie's understanding of the text differed from those of peers in its breadth and the depth of the description of the chairs, the richness and elaboration of the links reported and how Charlie inferred features in relation to the chairs.

Educators can observe high-level outcomes in multiple contexts. Two of the main contexts, achievement tests and open-ended tasks, are reviewed here.

Achievement tests

In this context, a student cohort responds to a set of achievement tasks in a particular domain. The tasks assess all students against a common set of benchmarks or criteria, that is, the tasks are 'convergent'. They frequently assess previously taught knowledge or skills and differ in difficulty or complexity. Schools frequently use standardised assessment scales here. One type is the timed multiple-choice achievement tests in a domain. These tests compare a school's outcomes with a reference 'typical' sample.

Students achieve high-level outcomes in this context by answering more of the tasks correctly in the allocated time. In Australia, this is typified by the National Assessment Program – Literacy and Numeracy (NAPLAN). Student outcomes on NAPLAN are assessed in several domains at 4 year levels. A student's score in each domain is reported in one of 4 'proficiency levels'. The 'exceeding' proficiency for each domain at each year level covers high ability and giftedness.

You can also get an impression of what high achievement and talent 'looks like' from the most difficult test items at each year level. On NAPLAN tests, typically, up to 30 per cent of students answer correctly the most difficult 10 per cent of items in each domain at each year level. These items illustrate the characteristics of high-level outcomes.

Other examples include the Progressive Achievement Tests in Reading, Mathematics, Science, STEM Contexts, Spelling, Punctuation and Grammar, as well as teacher-designed topic or domain tests.

These tests need to have sufficient items that assess comparatively high-level understanding or skills for the cohort as whole. Regular tests are often too easy for the high-ability and gifted students. Schools can use 'above-level', 'off-level' or 'out-of-level' tests that include tasks that are 2 to 5 year levels above the year of the regular students. These spread the scores of more capable learners and allow high-level outcomes to be identified.

Higher level test items can, for example, ask students to infer implications or possibilities, analyse and evaluate, compare, analogise, generalise or transfer their knowledge. They can require students to retain and manipulate more ideas. A teacher-designed year 3 reading comprehension task can include questions that require the use of comprehension skills or text knowledge that are typical of years 5 or 6.

Using higher level test items can identify a portion of those students capable of high-level outcomes. These items require students to have both the necessary domain knowledge and skill and the ability to display it in the 'window of opportunity' provided by the assessment task. This second requirement restricts high-level outcomes to those students who can 'play the assessment game successfully'. Test outcomes often indicate what a student knows about a predetermined set of ideas or skills. They do not necessarily tell you all that the student might know about a topic or how well a person can use a set of skills. For this, you need a more open-ended tool; that is, tasks that are less likely to restrict what a student can share with you.

Adaptive assessment

The online context offers a valuable opportunity for identifying high-level outcomes. The 'adaptive assessment' format is increasingly being used. This format adjusts the individual difficulty of items as each child progresses through the test. If a child consistently answers difficult questions correctly, the assessment program administers above-level, off-level or out-of-level tasks and can identify the most complex or difficult test items a student can answer correctly.

Rather than administering a set of test items in the same order to all students in a cohort, adaptive assessment selects a sequence of items that match each student's actual ability. The assessment monitors a student's initial set of responses during testing and automatically selects easier or more difficult tasks based on the student's performances so far. It continues to monitor the student's performance and adjust the difficulty of items accordingly. Instead of reporting a score that is related to a particular age or year range, adaptive assessments provide a score that is independent of these factors.

Assessment authorities are increasingly moving to adaptive assessment formats. Examples include the Australian Council for Educational Research's Progressive Achievement (PAT Adaptive) assessments in Reading and Mathematics and the Victorian Curriculum and Assessment Authority's Achievement tests in English and Numeracy.

Open-ended tasks

In this context, students respond to tasks that provide the opportunity to show all that they know or can do within a domain. They can do this by writing an extended text such as an essay, an argument, a theory or a narrative. They can prepare a spoken recording, use imagery, physical repertoires or concrete constructions that model their understanding and thinking. They can also engage in various types of problem-solving and research or investigative projects.

High-level outcomes in this context contain more than what the students were taught. Students can use it to show all that they know or believe at the time, how they believe the ideas are linked, their speculations about them, what they see as possibilities, their explanations of phenomena, alternative or creative perspectives on a topic and alternative options for achieving goals more efficiently or differently. The students can offer solutions to problems or challenges. Their productions in domains such as English, science, art, technology or music are novel or original and show evidence of thinking about topics in innovative and divergent ways.

These outcomes can indicate the extent or sophistication of a student's knowledge or skill about a topic. Some of the adjectives noted earlier can be used to describe the qualities of these outcomes; they can be 'atypical' and show an expert understanding, masterly control of the skills, original or creative interpretations and aspects that are unexpected.

The quality of the open-ended tasks can be evaluated and described using rubrics based on frameworks such as the Structure of Observed Learning Outcomes (SOLO) and Fischer's Dynamic Skill Theory (Mascolo and Fischer 2015). Some educators and schools feel uncomfortable about using open-ended tasks, in part because they believe that the outcomes cannot be assessed sufficiently objectively. Chapters 6 and 7 describe how schools can evaluate these outcomes.

What your school can do now

Students in your school are more likely to achieve high-level outcomes when your staff know what these 'look like' and how to allow for them to be achieved during regular teaching. The activities here guide your staff to negotiate a shared understanding of high-level outcomes.

Identify current staff knowledge and beliefs

What do staff currently know and believe about high-level outcomes? School leaders can start to address this question by inviting their staff to share their existing knowledge and beliefs. Activities can be used in which teachers reflect on, share, and negotiate their beliefs. These can include focus groups and surveys. Inadequate or incomplete understanding can slow down or restrict progress.

Negotiate criteria for high-level outcomes

Staff can review or evaluate their knowledge and beliefs about high-level outcomes. They can use the content in this chapter to update their understanding. They can negotiate a collaborative set of criteria for high-level outcomes. For example, high-level outcomes contain:

- comparatively high levels of sophistication and complexity in understanding
- unexpected meaningful relationships
- novel ways of solving problems and achieving goals and outcomes.

Identify high-level outcomes in teaching

Staff can use these criteria to decide what high-level outcomes might 'look like' for topics they will teach and how they will identify them in specific domains. They can also plan how they will implement the conditions that facilitate high-level outcomes. They can collect student responses that they think are instances of high-level outcomes and analyse them in collegiate discussions.

Develop a common language

School leaders can lead the development of a shared language for describing and discussing high-level outcomes. This can be achieved through negotiation with teachers, parents and carers and students. A common language gives the school a level of consistency in understanding, identifying and responding to high-level outcomes and in achieving its goals for optimal provision in this area.

Facilitate student opportunity

The school can now unpack how it will give students the opportunity to display high-level outcomes; for example, to show all that they know about a topic in assessment tasks. This includes informing students that these outcomes are expected and valued.

The student voice is an important contribution to improving provision here. Staff can examine whether and how they will ask students to evaluate the opportunities the students believe they have for displaying 'all that they know or can do' and how these opportunities could be modified.

Summary

High-level and talented outcomes:

- > are also referred to as 'advanced' or 'top of the range', and are ascribed the qualities of 'excellent', 'expert', 'masterly', 'original', 'creative', 'atypical' or 'unexpected'
- > come from students more comprehensively interpretating teaching and usually include ideas or content not mentioned explicitly in the teaching as well as unexpected or novel possibilities
- > can be displayed on achievement tests and on open-ended tasks and in problem-solving contexts
- > are usually in the top 15 to 25 per cent of outcomes for a cohort (talented outcomes fall in the top 10 per cent).

References

Gagné F (2020) *Differentiating giftedness from talent: the DMGT perspective on talent development*, Routledge, New York.

Griffiths A and Denton T (2013) *The 39-storey treehouse*, Treehouse series book 3, Pan Australia.

Harding SM, English N, Nibali N, Griffin P, Graham L, Alom B and Zhang Z (2019) 'Self-regulated learning as a predictor of mathematics and reading performance: a picture of students in Grades 5 to 8', *Australian Journal of Education*, 63(1):74–97, doi:10.1177/0004944119830153.

Mascolo MF and Fischer KW (2015) 'Dynamic development of thinking, feeling, and acting', in Overton WF, Molenaar P and Lerner RM (eds) *Handbook of child psychology and developmental science: theory and method*, Vol. 1, John Wiley & Sons, Inc.

CHAPTER 3

How do students achieve high-level outcomes?

Introduction

If schools are to foster and promote high-level outcomes, teachers need to know how students achieve these. When teachers are aware of the factors that lead to high-level outcomes, they can implement teaching and classroom cultures and climates that support them.

The main ideas in this chapter are shown in Figure 3.1.

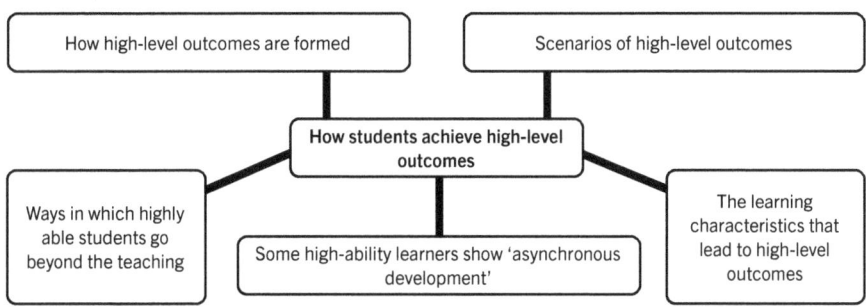

Figure 3.1. Achieving high-level outcomes in the classroom

How are high-level outcomes formed?

Students learn by interacting with the teaching information. They convert this information to new understanding and behavioural skills, and they link attitudes with the new knowledge. The outcomes we observe in the classroom come from this new understanding.

High-level outcomes come from high-ability understanding. Students who learn faster in a given time end up knowing more than their peers. They can learn faster because they have a more elaborated knowledge and can think about more ideas at any time. In their past, they have also learnt faster and have learnt more. As a consequence, they now have higher than average knowledge of particular topics.

Some students form an understanding encompassing more ideas than those presented in the teaching information. They do this by extending or inferring from the teaching content. They make links with parts of their knowledge that were not mentioned in the teaching and add these ideas to those in the teaching. This type of reasoning is called 'fluid analogising' (Geake 2008).

Scenarios

Bailey

An example of fluid analogising can be found in Bailey, a year 8 student in a class learning about how the human body digests food. Bailey's teacher described the journey of a hamburger, through the mouth, oesophagus, stomach and into the intestine. The teacher mentioned that the gastric juices in the stomach, including hydrochloric acid, break down protein foods, such as meat, eggs and milk. The teacher asked, 'Did anyone think of questions that I haven't mentioned?' Bailey replied, 'How do the glands in the wall of the stomach know how much acid to squirt out?' The teacher then asked, 'Why do you ask this question?'

Bailey explained, 'You said that too much acid could cause ulcers. Not enough wouldn't break down all the food. If I ate a hamburger today and a salad yesterday, my stomach would need different amounts of acid. I don't think I have ulcers in my stomach and so somehow my body controls it. Do my eyes work out how much acid I would need for food I will eat? Can you tell by chewing the food? Do you have detectors in your stomach to tell you?'

Bailey interpreted the teaching differently from her peers. Most formed an essentially literal understanding. Bailey went further, inferring 3 relationships from the teaching – that:

> digestion is a chemical reaction

> as a chemical reaction, it needs to be controlled

> this happens by managing or controlling how much of each chemical you have.

Bailey then synthesised these into a 'big idea' about digestion.

Chang

Chang, a year 2 student, gives us a second example. Chang's class read the story *Click clack moo: cows that type*. At the end of the story, the teacher asked, 'Why do you think the farmer refused the cows' request for electric blankets?'

Chang answered, 'Because he thought they might get burnt'. The teacher asked, 'Why do you think that?' Chang explained, 'You said that when electric blankets were first made some houses were burnt. You said typewriters stopped being used about 40 years ago. You said electric blankets were first made 50 years ago. The cows used the typewriter at the same time as when electric blankets were dangerous. That's why the farmer thought they might get burnt.'

Chang had formed a theory about the text by storing relationships from the text and linking them subjectively to infer relationships that were not in the text. Chang retained and thought in sophisticated ways about more ideas than typical of a year 2 student. This activity was done spontaneously; without external instruction.

Common features of Bailey and Chang's thinking

The understanding of the teaching information formed by these 2 students is typical of high-ability and gifted interpretations. 'Regular' peers generally learn what the teaching tells them. While some students may make low-level inferences that go beyond the teaching, the interpretations of Bailey and Chang go further. They include ideas from the teaching and additional ideas unique to each student.

Both students make links with other topics they know and add these to their understanding of the information. They infer patterns or relationships from this

> combination, analyse the patterns and synthesise them into 'big ideas'. They extend parts of the teaching to create a broader understanding. This activity occurs spontaneously; the teaching does not instruct the student to think in these ways.

High-ability students go beyond the teaching

Students differ in the extent to which they 'go beyond' the teaching. Some make small additions to the teaching. Others add substantially to the content and form 'hypotheses' or 'speculations' about it that go well beyond the teaching. Their understanding extends the content and often includes possibilities about other ideas in it.

The understanding highly able students form is a type of theory about what the teaching is saying. A theory is an interpretation of information that links facts and possibilities. The students' theories contain ideas that are linked into relationships. Their interpretations are referred to as 'intuitive' because the students may not yet have had the opportunity to test or evaluate some of these relationships; their interpretations are speculative.

These theories frequently include implicit questions that students can ask and the actions they can take to test their theories. Bailey's theory, for example, led her to question whether her eyes, chewing or stomach detectors indicated the amount of acid needed for the food Bailey was eating. The implicit questions or enquiries lead to actions the students can take. In other words, the intuitive theories are 'intuitive theories of action' or ITAs.

Students use a range of actions to research their theories. A student may ask questions that probe aspects of their theory. They may look for more information that could support it. They may physically experiment or take actions that evaluate possibilities that flow from it.

When students have the opportunity to research, analyse or evaluate their theories, they can modify and update them, converting them to more logical, tested theories. Such an understanding has more ideas in it than was in the teaching and is now validated. This leads to high-level outcomes.

High-ability and gifted students use these types of thinking spontaneously. They are not instructed by the teaching to think in these ways. Many children think like this from a very early age and learn more broadly and quickly than peers of the same age. This allows them to achieve higher outcomes on general intelligence or IQ tests. They teach themselves more knowledge by forming theories about information generally in their world, testing these theories, then updating their understanding.

However, such ways of thinking are not alone sufficient for forming higher level interpretations of the teaching. There are some students who have a more developed knowledge and think in these ways, but do not necessarily produce high-level outcomes. Students also need the emotional mindset and motivational orientation that will sustain this activity.

The teaching and curriculum need to provoke and challenge what students know (Dai 2017). The classroom environment needs to support their response to the challenges and provocations they form and give them the opportunity to explore and evaluate their intuitions. The school culture needs to explicitly encourage learning as the active pursuit of personal knowledge.

The student pathway to high-level outcomes can be represented as shown in Figure 3.2.

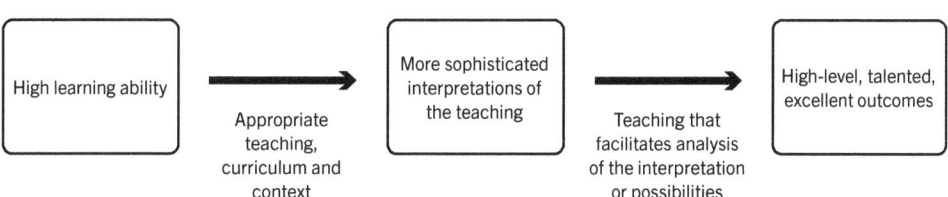

Figure 3.2. Student pathway to high-level outcomes

A high-ability and gifted learning profile

It is recommended that teachers and leaders be aware of how high-ability and gifted students achieve high-level outcomes and how their understanding changes as they interact with the teaching.

A high-ability or gifted learning profile encompasses a set of thinking characteristics typical of high-ability and gifted students. Students use these ways of thinking to help form their intuitive theories of the teaching that can lead in turn to high-level outcomes. They can also use them to interpret information about their world more generally and know it in these more sophisticated ways.

As noted earlier, having a high-ability and gifted profile on its own will not necessarily lead to students achieving high-level outcomes. The profile is the 'potential' for high-level outcomes, but the student's environment plays an important role. The environment needs to offer provocations that challenge what students know. It needs to support them to respond to challenges and provide them with the necessary tools and materials to do so. It also needs to show that it values the students' activity.

A high-ability or gifted learning profile is a precondition for achieving these outcomes. Without the various environmental conditions, however, it is less likely to lead to them. The cultural and contextual factors support the mapping of the high-ability and gifted learning profile into high-level outcomes.

Typical learning characteristics of a high-ability and gifted profile are outlined here.

Advanced domain knowledge

High-ability students have a better developed existing knowledge of the domain in which they form the high-level outcomes. They have a broader, more elaborated and differentiated set of concepts. This is indicated in the student's vocabulary. They can recall and apply this knowledge relatively easily, which helps them rapidly interpret the teaching information.

Complex thinking strategies

Students with high-ability and gifted learning profiles tend to use more complex thinking strategies and do this more flexibly and selectively. They shift between strategies more efficiently for complex problems (Carr et al. 1996). They infer, analyse, evaluate and synthesise meaningful relationships by linking ideas that seem unrelated to others spontaneously and independently. They cross 'topic boundaries' and make analogies between topics or use 'far transfer' thinking (Geake 2008; Preusse 2011). This allows them to link ideas in novel, lateral, unexpected ways.

Ability to synthesise high-level understanding

As well as being able to link ideas in complex, more efficient ways, high-ability and gifted students draw in a wider range of ideas and incorporate these into a broader understanding. They synthesise, organise and re-organise the ideas in their new understanding in more complex ways, often in a 'big ideas' way. They form subjective patterns and personal 'rules' about the information (Rizza et al. 2001). These become their 'intuitive theories' about the teaching. Their understanding of a topic has been described as showing the characteristics of expertise (Munro 2013) and wisdom (Sternberg 2013).

Efficient working memory retention

High-ability students are also often able to chunk teaching information more efficiently. They retain more ideas in their thinking spaces or working memories at once (Rodríguez et al. 2019), think in larger jumps or 'chunks' of knowledge and keep track of multiple ideas or aspects of a topic (Kornmann et al. 2015). This helps them form interpretations that have more concepts or ideas. They can show enhanced working memories for verbal and imagery knowledge (Ogurlu 2020).

Advanced metacognition and self-regulation

High-ability students tend to manage, monitor and direct their learning activity spontaneously and more efficiently. They use self-regulation and metacognitive strategies more efficiently (Alonso 1999; Carr et al. 1996; Weil et al. 2013). They often don't wait to be told how to think by the teaching; they are more 'self-programming' rather than being 'programmed externally' by the teaching.

Innovative problem-solving

It is also common for high-ability and gifted students to ask complex questions about ideas and to solve problems in unusual or novel ways (Maker 2005; Maker et al. 2015).

Strong imagination

The novel approach of high-ability and gifted students extends to imagination and creativity. They frequently use imagination or fantasy and often show 'intellectual playfulness' (Smith and Mathur 2009).

High enthusiasm and curiosity

High-ability students also have the emotional infrastructure or 'learning personality' needed to learn independently when given the opportunity. The intensity of the emotion these students invest in learning has been described as 'overexcitability' (Piechowski 1986). They can:

- show focused, intense interest in a topic as well as enthusiasm and cognitive curiosity
- be self-motivated to think and learn about the topic and show high intrinsic motivation for excellence
- have a higher self-concept and believe they can successfully 'go alone beyond the teaching'
- show task commitment, focus, endurance and persistence with difficult tasks; respond positively to barriers; show personal standards of intellectual activity and creativity (Worrell and Erwin 2011)
- believe that their peers and teacher can be trusted with their 'untaught' ideas and will respect them (Fox et al. 2010; Gagné 2009; Ogurlu 2020; Subotnik et al. 2011).

The display of these cognitive emotions at any time depends on the extent to which the students perceive a supportive environment.

Philosophical personality

The final characteristic described here is that high-ability and gifted students tend to operate as 'intuitive philosophers'. They reflect on their learning and social interactions and form an identity as an individual who learns 'differently' from peers; they develop their 'personal theory' of intelligence (Hsueh 1997). They are more aware of what they know and how they learn. They set themselves goals for learning, respond to challenges and reduce uncertainty about their world (Fox et al. 2010). They show a personality disposition that is characterised by heightened intuition, thinking and perceiving (Sak 2004).

Asynchronous development in high-ability and gifted learners

Some high-ability and gifted learners show 'asynchronous development'; that is, some aspects of their learning profile develop more rapidly than others. This leads to a discrepancy or gap that can affect their overall learning. Some students, for example, show high-level domain knowledge and immature emotional stability or social interaction skills with their peer group. Three typical examples of this discrepancy based on Neihart's (2002) categories of gifted learning profiles are:

> - Some students don't know how to share their understanding successfully with their same-age peers. They may be rejected or bullied by their peers and often prefer to communicate with adults or older, 'like-thinking' students.
> - Some try to hide their higher understanding and knowing, fearing the consequences of sharing their knowledge and how they think.
> - Some are disengaged or alienated from classroom culture and can show negative emotional responses to the classroom.

This asynchronous development restricts how these students engage in the classroom. Teachers can attribute these behaviour patterns to the students being loners, uncooperative, disinterested, lazy, unmotivated or having behavioural or personality issues.

Teachers need to understand the influences of asynchronous development and have ways of responding effectively. They need to understand how these affect the interaction between the student's high-ability and gifted learning profile and the classroom culture and climate.

What your school can do now

Your school is more likely to have students achieve high-level outcomes when your staff can recognise, scaffold and support high-ability and gifted learning profiles in their teaching. This includes recognising these students' intuitive theories of action and implementing the environmental and cultural supports for these outcomes. Recommended follow-up activities are outlined here.

Scaffold understanding of high-ability and gifted profiles

School leaders can scaffold staff's awareness of students' intuitive theories of action stemming from the teaching in their classrooms. Staff can infer what these might look like in topics they will teach and identify them by understanding students' interpretations of and responses to the teaching.

Staff can also look for evidence of emotional mindsets and motivational orientations that lead to high-level outcomes.

Recognise high-ability and gifted learning profiles

Teachers can be encouraged to collect and analyse instances in which they think students are forming intuitive theories of action. They can then compare the knowledge in the student's interpretations with the teaching information and note how the student has added to it. Recordings of these episodes can be shared and unpacked with colleagues. You can prepare and equip your staff to make these evaluations by using the following activity, where staff:

> ❯ infer what high-ability and gifted thinking would 'look like' in content they teach

> describe how they could evaluate students' responses as they learn the content

> unpack what they would see as evidence of the types of thinking in students' responses as they learn.

Staff can negotiate collaboratively their understanding of high learning ability and giftedness. The activities discussed in this section provide teachers with the data needed to develop agreed definitions of high learning ability and giftedness. This will inform the school's code of teaching practice and provide the basis for identification of these students.

Summary

> High-ability students link the message in the teaching with other areas of their knowledge to form high-level interpretations that are 'intuitive theories of action'.

> They do this by using their 'high-ability and gifted learning profile' or 'learning potential'; this comprises their advanced knowledge, high-level thinking strategies, emotional mindset and motivational orientation.

> High-ability students' learning profile alone is insufficient to form talented outcomes. They also need supportive environmental and cultural conditions. This includes the appropriate teaching and curriculum that provokes and challenges learning and a classroom environment that scaffolds the opportunity to explore and evaluate their intuitions.

> Some high-ability and gifted learners show 'asynchronous development'; some aspects of their learning profile develop more rapidly than others. This leads to a discrepancy that can affect their overall learning.

References

Alonso E (1999) *A meta-analysis of the metacognition of gifted children* [unpublished doctoral dissertation], Miami Institute of Psychology.

Carr M, Alexander J and Schwanenflugel P (1996) 'Where gifted children do and do not excel on metacognitive tasks', *Roeper Review*, 18(3):212–217, doi:10.1080/02783199609553740.

Dai DY (2017) 'Envisioning a new foundation for gifted education: evolving complexity theory (ECT) of talent development', *Gifted Child Quarterly*, 61(3):172–182, doi:10.1177/0016986217701837.

Fox E, Dinsmore DL and Alexander PA (2010) 'Reading competence, interest, and reading goals in three gifted young adolescent readers', *High Ability Studies*, 21(2):165–178, doi:10.1080/13598139.2010.525340.

Gagné F (2010) 'Motivation within the DMGT 2.0 framework', *High Ability Studies*, 21(2):81–99, doi:10.1080/13598139.2010.525341.

Geake JG (2008) High abilities at fluid analogizing: a cognitive neuroscience construct of giftedness, *Roeper Review*, 30(3):187–195, doi:10.1080/02783190802201796.

Hsueh WC (1997) *A cross-cultural comparison of gifted children's theories of intelligence, goal orientation and responses to challenge* [unpublished Ph.D. dissertation], Purdue University, Indiana.

Kornmann J, Zettler I, Kammerer Y, Gerjets P and Trautwein U (2015) 'What characterizes children nominated as gifted by teachers? A closer consideration of working memory and intelligence', *High Ability Studies*, 26(1):75–92, doi:10.1080/13598139.2015.1033513.

Maker CJ (2005) *The DISCOVER Project: improving assessment and curriculum for diverse gifted learners*, The National Research Center on the Gifted and Talented, University of Connecticut, Storrs, CT, accessed 27 October 2023. https://nrcgt.uconn.edu/newsletters/fall053/

Maker CJ, Zimmerman R, Gomez-Arizaga MP, Pease R and Burke EM (2015) 'Developing real-life problem solving: integrating the DISCOVER problem matrix, problem-based learning, and thinking actively in a social context', in Vidergor HE and Harris CR (eds) *Applied practice for educators of gifted and able learners*, Sense Publishers, Rotterdam.

Munro J (2013) 'Gifted students as expert+ knowers: a teaching friendly model of gifted knowing and understanding?', *CSE Seminar Series*, Seminar Paper 225, Centre for Strategic Education, East Melbourne.

Neihart M (2002) 'Risk and resilience in gifted children: a conceptual framework', in Neihart M, Reis SM, Robinson NM and Moon SM (eds) *The social and emotional development of gifted children: what do we know?*, Prufrock Press, Waco, TX.

Ogurlu U (2020) 'Overview of meta-analyses on giftedness', *Gifted and Talented International*, 35(2):110–127, doi:10.1080/15332276.2021.1893135.

Piechowski MM (1986) 'The concept of developmental potential', *Roeper Review*. 8(3):190–97, doi:10.1080/02783198609552971.

Preusse F, Van Der Meer E, Deshpande G, Krueger F and Wartenburger I (2011) 'Fluid intelligence allows flexible recruitment of the parieto-frontal network in analogical reasoning', *Frontiers in Human Neuroscience*, 5(22):1–14, doi:10.3389/fnhum.2011.00022.

Rizza MG, McIntosh DE and McCunn A (2001) 'Profile analysis of the Woodcock-Johnson III tests of cognitive abilities with gifted students', *Psychology in the Schools*, 38(5):447–455, doi:10.1002/pits.1033.

Rodríguez Naveiras E, Verche Borges E, Hernández Lastiri P, Montero López R and Borges Del Rosal MÁ (2019) 'Differences in working memory between gifted or talented students and community samples: a meta-analysis', *Psicothema*, 31(3):255–262, doi:10.7334/psicothema2019.18.

Sak U (2004) 'A synthesis of research on psychological types of gifted adolescents', *Journal of Secondary Gifted Education*, 15(2):70–79, doi:10.4219/jsge-2004-449.

Smith M and Mathur R (2009) 'Children's imagination and fantasy: implications for development, education, and classroom activities', *Research in the Schools*, 16(1):52–63.

Sternberg RJ (2013) 'Wisdom, intelligence, creativity, synthesised: a model of giftedness', in Balchin T, Hymer B and Matthews DJ (eds) *The Routledge international companion to gifted education*, 1st edn, Routledge.

Subotnik RF, Olszewski-Kubilius P and Worrell FC (2011) 'Rethinking giftedness and gifted education: a proposed direction forward based on psychological science', *Psychological Science in the Public Interest*, 12(1):3–54, doi:10.1177/1529100611418056.

Weil LG, Fleming SM, Dumontheil I, Kilford EJ, Weil RS, Rees G, Dolan RJ and Blakemore SJ (2013) 'The development of metacognitive ability in adolescence', *Consciousness and Cognition*, 22(1):264–271, doi:10.1016/j.concog.2013.01.004.

Worrell FC and Erwin JO (2011) 'Best practices in identifying students for gifted and talented education programs', *Journal of Applied School Psychology*, 27(4):319–340, doi:10.1080/15377903.2011.615817.

CHAPTER 4

What do multiple high-ability and gifted learning profiles look like?

Introduction

There are multiple high-ability and gifted learning profiles. Educational provision, however, does not typically cater for all of these. Consequently, not all students with high-ability and gifted learning profiles receive equitable opportunities for generating high-level outcomes. Educators need to know how to recognise and accommodate a range of high-ability and gifted learning profiles.

Educators and researchers differ in the types of gifted learning profile they identify. Some identify 2 types of gifted profiles and others identify 3. Betts and Neihart (1988) identify 6 profiles, 3 of which refer to students who have, in addition, a second learning exceptionality. This book identifies 3 major profiles: verbal, imagery and performance. These are described in this chapter in terms of how students with each profile interpret teaching information and the qualities of the intuitive theories the students form.

The main ideas in this chapter are shown in Figure 4.1.

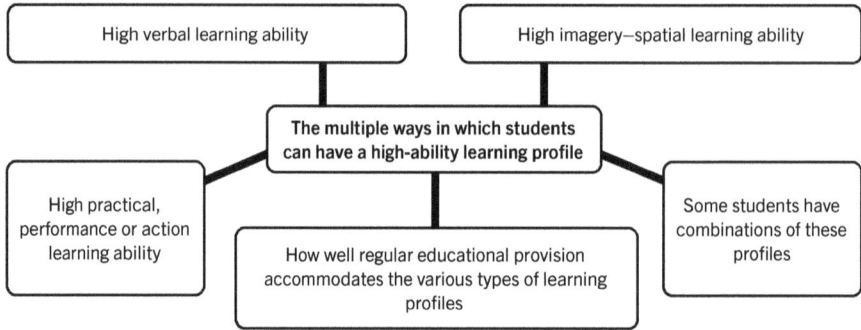

Figure 4.1. Multiple forms of high-ability and gifted learning profiles

High verbal learning ability

One type of information from which we learn is text-like information. All texts use the same features to convey meaning, whether a film, a written narrative, a painting, a conversation, a game of football, a dramatic play or a plumbing routine.

Any text is made up of several types of meaning. First, it has meanings of individual items, such as details, concepts or vocabulary. These are linked and sequenced into relationships, which are sentence-like meanings. These in turn are linked into larger meanings, such as paragraphs, and organised around a topic or theme. Each text also has a genre that is formed by using agreed conventions and a purpose.

Most students, when exposed to a text, form an interpretation of its message. Others go beyond this. They infer the direction in which it is going by linking it with other texts they have learnt. They infer additional details and possibilities the text might mention. They synthesise their understanding of the text and their inferred ideas into intuitive theories about the text. These theories are more elaborated and extensive than those of typical learners and lead to talented comprehension, production and use of the text. In addition, these students are often fast learners in the classroom. They quickly infer the direction and topic of the teaching and seem to be 'one step ahead' of it. They have an advanced vocabulary and use language competently across contexts. They do well on tests and tasks.

Verbal giftedness can be shown for texts in all subject areas. All domains have texts. The texts can be spoken or written or they can be represented visually, diagrammatically or in action sequences. They include the symbolic systems in mathematics, in musical compositions, in information technology and in sport. An art student may learn a genre of painting, reflect on it, wonder about modifying it to communicate differently and extend the genre. An information technology student may learn to design apps using particular algorithms, speculate about modifying them and extend the functionality of the apps they were taught. A history student might apply ideas from ancient Egypt to early Asian cultures and discover other influences on the development of the Asian cultures. Gifted textual or verbal thinking can lead to intuitive theories and talented outcomes in all subject areas. It is not restricted to English, but verbal high ability and giftedness is domain specific. Being gifted in one domain doesn't guarantee high ability and giftedness in others. Texts in different domains use different types of meanings. Art texts have different meanings from music, mathematics, information technology or English texts.

This type of gifted learning profile has also been called 'academic giftedness'. It matches or is synonymous with 'school-house' giftedness (Renzulli 2012), 'knowledge consuming' giftedness (Tannenbaum 1987) and 'analytical' giftedness (Sternberg 2005).

In other words, this profile refers to an advanced ability to think about ideas abstractly.

Scenario

Reza

Reza was solving year 12 calculus problems at age 6. Reza never attended regular school, was home-schooled by parents who were not interested in maths and was self-taught in mathematics using teaching information from the Khan Academy.

Reza's ability to form intuitive theories is shown here. Reza had learnt about quadratic and cubic polynomials, including how to draw graphs typified by $y = x^2 - 5x + 6$ and $y = x^3 - 4x^2 + 3x - 2$. The teacher asked if it was possible to draw polynomials to the power of x^7 or x^8. Although never having been taught to draw these graphs, without hesitation Reza drew graphs typified by $y = x^7 - 3x^3 + 6$ and $y = x^8 - 4x^3 + 3x^2 - 2$. Reza's intuitive theory about polynomials allowed the inference of patterns and for Reza to think in a 'big ideas' way about them.

Reza also had severe social and emotional issues and had few friends, experiencing difficulty tolerating and interacting with same-age peers. Reza perceived many situations in life to be threatening, in part because of the thought of possible endangering consequences. Because of these perceived threats, Reza displayed broad-based anxiety and withdrawal. This in turn restricted the opportunity to learn age-appropriate social interaction skills.

High imagery–spatial learning ability

Students with an imagery-spatial learning profile link with experiences they have stored in memory. Ideas in an experience are linked in images, in time and in space. Some students think at a high level by manipulating images and spatial and temporal information. They infer that the present situation is similar to or matches seemingly unrelated earlier experiences in some ways. This is an example of making 'fluid analogies' or 'far transfer'. The students apply ideas from the earlier experiences to the present experience and combine them to form intuitive theories of action (Martin-Ordas et al. 2014). Their interpretations of teaching are broader and make links with ideas they know, which are not mentioned in the teaching; they 'go beyond' it.

Experiences are personal. The intuitive theories these students form are unique to them. They see shared features and possibilities that other people don't see. Becoming aware of possibilities leads to outcomes that are more creative, lateral or unusual. This profile has been displayed by great scientists and inventors such as Einstein, great authors such as Agatha Christie, great artists such as van Gogh and great politicians such as Winston Churchill. West's (2013) *In the mind's eye* provides many other examples.

This type of giftedness has been called 'visual–spatial' giftedness (Silverman 2002). The term 'imagery–spatial' is used because these students are not restricted to visual images; they can also think about auditory images in context. This matches Renzulli's (2012) 'creative-productive giftedness', Tannenbaum's (1987) 'producers of knowledge' and Sternberg's (2005) 'creative intelligence'.

In summary, this profile refers to an advanced ability to think about ideas in imagery or space-and-time ways.

Scenario

Aaliyah

A year 3 class was learning about mini beasts. They watched a colony of slaters scurrying away when a rock in the playground was rolled over. The teacher asked, 'Has anyone thought of something I haven't mentioned?' Aaliyah responded, 'How many toes does a slater have?' The teacher asked, 'Why do you ask that?' Aaliyah showed the length of a slater using 2 forefingers and said, 'They are this long, and they run very fast. My Little Aths coach told me that if I want to go fast, I must push back with my big toe. The slaters must have big toes.' Aaliyah visualised the slaters with comparatively large 'beetle toes' and then formed other speculations: 'Perhaps they breathe much faster and change it into energy'.

How can we unpack this student's thinking? Aaliyah linked the present experience of the slaters moving with an experience at Little Athletics and then transferred this to the slaters' context. This led to the intuitive theory that slaters' speed could be due to their toes. Comparatively, 'big toes' was a possible explanation of the rapid speed of beetles.

This was typical of Aaliyah's responses to teaching information. Aaliyah regularly showed thinking that was lateral or 'outside the square', did not move in the direction of the teaching and asked unusual or unexpected questions. Aaliyah looked at situations from a 'big ideas' perspective, analysed them at a high level and manipulated several aspects of a situation at once. These learning behaviours suggested a creative imagination; yet Aaliyah was also not good at learning conventions such as phonics or spelling rules and did not engage well with repetitive tasks.

High practical performance or action learning ability

This type of giftedness is often devalued or even discouraged in schools. These students think in terms of actions or 'doing' at an advanced level. They infer how a set of actions that works in one situation can be modified to work in other situations to lead to creative, innovative or talented outcomes. The actions may be about how to use paint, a musical instrument, gymnastic movements, a science or technology tool, how to kick, hit or throw a ball, or how to apply information technology to solve problems. These students have tacit or implicit knowledge about contexts (Sternberg 2005).

The knowledge and understanding formed by these students is often not taught formally or explicitly. In classrooms where practical performance high-ability and gifted students are not understood or where the advanced quality in their interpretations is not recognised, high-level outcomes may be restricted. Many adults who display talented outcomes that are based on this profile report feelings of dissatisfaction with, rejection of, and alienation from their school experiences (West 2013). This is unpacked in more depth in the next chapter.

In summary, this profile refers to an advanced ability to think about ideas in practical ways, using actions. This leads to high performance outcomes.

Scenarios

Siddarth

A year 1 class took an excursion to a display of old-fashioned steam-driven tractors. The owner of one of the tractors explained how it worked. The teacher took photos of some of the tractors as a record.

Back in the classroom, the children were asked to draw a picture of what they had learnt. Most children drew typical year 1–level pictures. Siddarth's drawing was different. It not only showed the detailed parts of a tractor, but also the sequence of steps from the wood in the firebox to the piston moving the wheels. The students hadn't seen this happening; they had only heard a brief description. Siddarth's picture showed that he guessed that the piston was circular inside the cylinder. Siddarth explained how the piston moved backwards and forwards by having the steam 'take turns going into the cylinder at both ends'.

Rory

Rory is a year 10 student who has been interested in computers from a young age. Rory began constructing and selling internet computer games at age 9, creating and selling encryption codes and designing training programs that teach individuals how to improve their online gaming skill.

Common features of Siddarth and Rory's thinking

These students thought in actions at a high level. Siddarth inferred and synthesised the set of actions into an intuitive theory about how to propel a steam tractor. Rory thought of the actions that could be used to solve problems in online gaming activity and formed an intuitive theory about how an online game might work. They both synthesised and used action sequences to solve problems in real-life contexts.

Combination high-ability and gifted profiles

Some students have 2 of these profiles or all 3. They can switch, for example, from thinking in the 'high-ability verbal way' to the 'imagery way'. The intuitive theories of these students are generally richer than those of students who have one gifted profile. Some educators and researchers combine the high-ability imagery–spatial and practical performance profiles into a 'non-verbal' category.

Does regular educational provision accommodate the varied learning profiles?

Of the range of high-ability and gifted learning profiles, the verbal profile is most likely to be accommodated in regular teaching. Conventional classrooms are essentially verbal contexts that require students to learn by listening, speaking, reading and writing. Verbal presentations and texts are used to teach in all curriculum domains.

The imagery–spatial profile is not usually targeted by regular teaching. The intuitive understanding of these students is often unusual and unexpected and may question the teaching. Educators frequently don't know how to interpret these students' responses or how to scaffold and guide students to map their abilities into high-level outcomes. The action or practical high-ability and gifted profile is also not usually targeted by regular teaching. High-level 'street wise' learning ability, advanced problem-solving ability or innovative action ability in practical, everyday contexts often isn't valued in the classroom.

Students with the imagery or practical learning profiles often do not get the opportunity to convert their high learning capacity into high-level outcomes. As a consequence, these students often disengage from regular teaching and may show behavioural or social issues (Lakin and Wai 2020).

Some high-ability and gifted students have difficulty showing and sharing what they know in the conventional ways provided in regular education. Regular provision may require a level of proficiency in literacy or numeracy and these students may underachieve. They are referred to as 'twice exceptional'; they have both a high-ability and gifted learning profile and they underachieve. These students and teaching procedures to assist them are discussed in Chapters 5 and 6.

What your school can do now

Many schools focus on recognising and supporting the traditionally 'academic' high-level learning outcomes. This book believes that there are advantages for individual students and the school when the range of high-ability and gifted learning profiles is identified and fostered. The outcomes from students who have imagery or practical high-ability and gifted profiles are creative and innovative and can enhance the knowledge and understanding of the general student cohort.

This section considers a school's awareness of the multiple ways in which students can be highly able and the extent that it:

- > recognises instances of these profiles
- > identifies students who display the varied high-ability and gifted learning profiles
- > implements teaching and curriculum that allows these students to realise high-level outcomes.

Some recommended follow-up activities are discussed here.

Recognise varied high-ability and gifted learning profiles

What do your staff know about the range of high-ability and gifted learning profiles? They will be more able to recognise and foster multiple profiles when they know what they 'look like'. School leaders can guide staff to recall students they have encountered who:

- > interpreted the teaching at a high level but linked the ideas in unusual, quirky ways or who raised unexpected possibilities
- > seemed to have high-level imagery or practical understanding of ideas but not verbal academic understanding and who possibly achieved at a high level in domains outside the classroom
- > learnt in unconventional ways.

Staff can re-evaluate these experiences and the learning behaviours these students displayed from the perspective of the range of learning profiles.

Evaluate identification criteria

Which students does your school identify as having high learning ability? Are some profiles preferred or prioritised over others? Staff can analyse and evaluate the criteria, explicit and implicit, used by the school and by their teaching to identify a high-ability and gifted profile.

Reflect on assumptions

What opportunity does your school provide for students with a range of high-ability and gifted profiles to form high-level outcomes? All teaching, by necessity, makes assumptions about how students learn. These assumptions can inadvertently limit the opportunity some students have to achieve high-level outcomes.

School leaders can encourage teachers to reflect on the assumptions they make about high-ability and gifted learning profiles and to decide whether some may be prioritised or preferenced and others neglected or excluded by teaching practice.

Summary

> There are multiple high-ability and gifted learning profiles: high verbal, high imagery–spatial and high practical or action learning ability.

> Some students have high learning ability in 2 or all 3 of these areas.

> The high verbal learning ability profile is most likely to be accommodated in regular teaching.

> Students with high imagery–spatial or practical profiles often don't have their intuitive theories valued by educators or get the opportunity to map them into high-level outcomes. They often disengage from regular teaching and may show behavioural or social issues.

References

Betts GT and Neihart M (1988) 'Profiles of the gifted and talented', *Gifted Child Quarterly*, 32(2):248–253, doi:10.1177/001698628803200202.

Lakin JM and Wai J (2020) 'Spatially gifted, academically inconvenienced: spatially talented students experience less academic engagement and more behavioural issues than other talented students', *British Journal of Educational Psychology*, 90(4):1015–1038, doi:10.1111/bjep.12343.

Martin-Ordas G, Atance CM and Caza JS (2014) 'How do episodic and semantic memory contribute to episodic foresight in young children?', *Frontiers in Psychology*, 5:732, doi:10.3389/fpsyg.2014.00732.

Renzulli JS (2012) 'Re-examining the role of gifted education and talent development for the 21st century: a four-part theoretical approach', *Gifted Child Quarterly,* 56(3):150–159, doi:10.1177/0016986212444901

Shavinina LV (2013) *The Routledge international handbook of innovation education*, Taylor and Francis, Hoboken.

Sternberg RJ (2005) 'The WICS model of giftedness', in Sternberg RJ and Davidson JE (eds) *Conceptions of giftedness,* 2nd edn, Cambridge University, West Nyack, NY.

Sternberg RJ (2006) 'Practical giftedness', *Gifted Education International*, 21(2–3):89–98, doi:10.1177/026142940602100303.

Tannenbaum AJ (1987) *Gifted children: psychological and educational perspectives*, Macmillan, New York.

West TG (2013) *In the mind's eye: visual thinkers, gifted people with dyslexia and other learning difficulties, computer images and the ironies of creativity*, Prometheus Books, New York.

CHAPTER 5

Twice-exceptional students

Introduction

Before leaving the discussion of the different learning profiles, another group should be accounted for. These are students who have high learning ability but who underachieve at school. You may have had experiences with students who were gifted and had dyslexia, highly able students who were autistic or students from minority cultures who were creative and innovative but didn't achieve at a high level academically.

The main ideas in this chapter are shown in Figure 5.1.

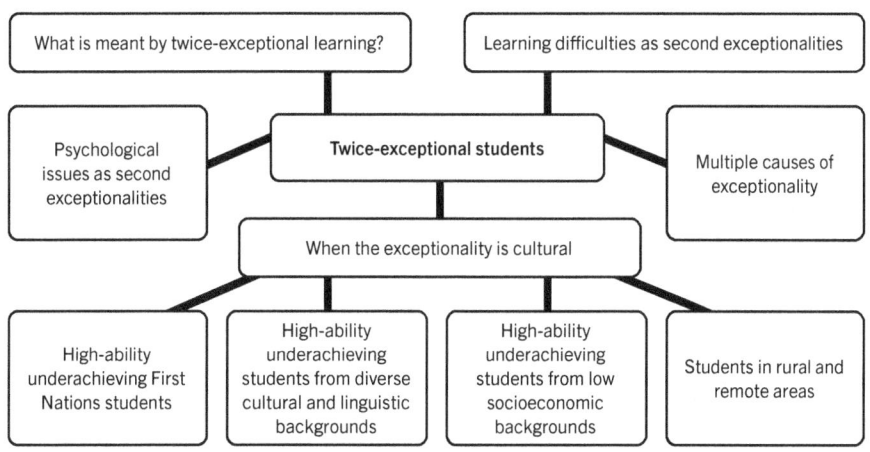

Figure 5.1. Twice-exceptional students

What is meant by twice-exceptional learning?

Biographies (for example, West 2013) tell us that many of the famous individuals who have made great contributions to our world had learning exceptionalities. They showed evidence of their second exceptionality in how they interacted with their worlds. Albert Einstein had dyslexia and dyscalculia, Charles Darwin had Asperger's syndrome, Agatha Christie had dysgraphia, George Washington and Pablo Picasso had dyslexia, Leonardo da Vinci had dyslexia, ADHD and other learning disorders and attention issues.

In the classroom, twice-exceptional students show a discrepancy between high learning ability or potential and outcomes. They show high-level outcomes occasionally and usually unexpectedly. Their learning profiles are perplexing in their lack of consistency. Their 'flashes of brilliance' are difficult to predict. On most occasions, their outcomes are average at best. They may seem to be lazy, unmotivated, socially isolated, withdrawn, disengaged or disruptive.

The second exceptionality can mask the student's high learning capacity and restrict their ability to achieve high-level outcomes at school. The exceptionality can be emotional, social, cultural or cognitive and often leads to academic underachievement, social and behavioural problems and disengagement from regular classroom participation. Gifted students in this category are referred to as 'twice exceptional', 'dual exceptional' or 'gifted underachievers'.

The influence of the second exceptionality on learning can be exacerbated when regular classroom teaching doesn't recognise it and is not differentiated or modified to take account of it. Regular teaching is often expository; it expects students to learn by being informed or told. It assumes students learn by being 'programmed externally' and may use 'rote-type' procedures.

As noted in Chapter 3, high-ability and gifted students frequently learn by looking for the meaning in a context, rather than by 'being told'. They are more 'self-programming' learners. They do need to learn by being programmed externally, but this needs to be aligned and balanced with their advanced ability to learn by looking for meaning and by forming intuitive theories of action.

This category includes high-ability and gifted students who also have academic learning difficulties, those who have psychological issues and those from diverse cultural or environmental backgrounds that do not match the tacit assumptions made by the teaching.

It should be noted that professionals in this area differ in how they define twice-exceptional and gifted underachieving students. Some see them as different categories, some see the twice-exceptional category as included within the gifted underachiever category, and others use the 2 terms synonymously. This book uses the 2 terms synonymously.

A checklist for identifying twice-exceptional students has been developed by the Institute for the Study of Advanced Development (2019).

Twice-exceptional learning scenarios

These scenarios illustrate the complexity of twice exceptionality in the classroom. The main types and causes are unpacked in the sections that follow.

Prim

Prim is in year 4 and is advanced in understanding what is being taught, showing creativity, curiosity and humour. Prim's ability to recall accounts and experiences is very high. This includes explanations, factual details and narratives.

Prim has high-level social interaction skills and a strong sense of social justice, actively supporting peers when it seems they are being treated inappropriately. Prim becomes intensely concerned when observing children being treated unjustly on the news and spontaneously planned and led a fundraising campaign in class for children suffering from hunger in Africa.

Prim's second exceptionality is in literacy learning, with reading comprehension scores consistently in the lowest 20 percentile range in the year and word reading and spelling scores in the lowest 10 percentile range. Prim's writing comprises very short sentences, basic vocabulary and few elaborations or descriptions, showing none of depth and richness evident in Prim's spoken language. Prim's maths outcomes, on the other hand, have consistently been in the top 10 percentile range.

As Prim continues in education, there will be an increasing requirement to learn by using appropriate literacy skills. Teachers and parents have already observed that Prim delays engaging with tasks that require reading or writing, appears to drown in the information and gives up quickly. Prim progresses through tasks relatively slowly and laboriously, taking much longer than peers to complete them. Prim displays these difficulties in all domains, including those that are enjoyable, and finds these experiences frustrating and anxiety arousing.

Jo

Jo in year 7 was referred for a psychoeducational assessment because of academic underachievement and the range of autism spectrum disorder and ADHD behaviours displayed in the classroom. Jo is easily distressed by the teaching or environmental information and contorts their body, flaps their hands, pulls their hair or begins to shout or cry. Jo does not have any friends and spends recess and lunch times alone, wandering the playground, talking to themself.

During the psychoeducational assessment, Jo had difficulty remaining seated and engaging with the tasks. Jo was easily distracted and frequently requested water and permission to go to the toilet. Jo's verbal and non-verbal IQ scores were at the 19th and 22nd percentiles respectively and literacy and numeracy outcomes were in the lowest 10 percentile range. When the assessor showed Jo a previously unseen LEGO kit, Jo engaged with it intently and completed it without interruption in 40 minutes. The self-talk Jo used while working through it showed a range of high-level thinking skills.

Jo has displayed outstanding achievements at school. The art teacher assessed Jo's outcomes as excellent, with sculptures of humans engaged in moving that were 'vital, dynamic and exceptional' for Jo's age. The drama teacher marveled at Jo's consistent ability to use movement sequences to elicit sophisticated emotions. Jo's knowledge of botany and biology is largely self-taught, advanced and sophisticated.

Narry

Narry is a year 9 student at a large suburban high school, who is a conundrum and a frustration to classroom teachers. Narry thinks rapidly, but not in the ways that would help academic advancement. Narry has excellent knowledge of a range of subjects, but this doesn't seem to help with academic success. Specialist teachers report that Narry shows advanced aptitude in information technology, physical education and music classes.

In classroom discussions, Narry's contributions are creative and interesting but unexpected, showing links between ideas that peers miss or do not understand. On excursions, Narry can be relied on to see ways around obstacles that arise.

Narry's recall of factual knowledge and writing and spelling ability, on the other hand, are extremely low. Teachers are also concerned that Narry often appears to daydream or doodle, does not follow instructions on completing assignments and is disorganised in study and homework activity.

A psychoeducational assessment indicated that Narry's verbal reasoning was at the 64th percentile and non-verbal reasoning at the 99th percentile. Narry's reading comprehension, writing and spelling scores were at the 13th, 4th, and 8th percentiles respectively. Analytic sequential processing was at the 17th percentile, academic self-efficacy was at the 14th percentile and academic motivation to learn was at the 9th percentile.

At home, Narry works on self-generated projects, dismantling computers and appliances and combining the parts to make new devices. One of Narry's creations was awarded first place in a science fair competition. Narry's regular teachers and other students were very impressed, as they had not seen evidence of that kind of performance from Narry before.

Learning difficulties as second exceptionalities

Participation in regular classroom learning usually requires the use of literacy and numeracy skills. Some students with a high learning ability have difficulty learning these skills. Some have difficulty reading or spelling words correctly or displaying their knowledge by writing. Some have difficulty learning to use foundational maths skills, such as counting or deciding the number of items in a quantity.

These difficulties are attributed to specific cognitive processes used to interpret information (Gartin and Murdick 2005). Literacy learning difficulties by high-ability and gifted students, for example, have been attributed to a difficulty breaking spoken words into separate sounds and linking them in the correct sequence (Munro 2005).

Similarly, maths learning difficulties can be attributed to a difficulty breaking a quantity into separate units and giving each unit a separate number name.

Lim (2021) found that twice-exceptional students were similar to regular learning peers with learning difficulties on lower-order skills, such as decoding and maths computations, and more like high-ability peers on higher-order skills, such as advanced verbal comprehension.

These twice-exceptional students had difficulty analysing information into smaller parts and then linking the parts in the intended sequence. This is an example of 'analytic sequential' thinking. These students often also show this sequencing difficulty on other tasks; for example, working memory and processing speed tasks on some intelligence tests (Assouline et al. 2010; Lim 2021).

Twice-exceptional students with a learning difficulty frequently use the alternative to analytic sequential thinking. This is 'synthetic-wholistic' thinking (Koo et al. 2018). It involves inferring the overall meaning or context of the information by using the relationships between parts and integrating them rather than sequencing them. This equips them to learn in larger steps and more rapidly (Beekman and Seo 2021). However, they can also ignore or neglect relevant detail and develop 'unique' or 'subjective' rather than 'taught' ways of thinking and acting. While most students use both types of thinking in a balanced way, some twice-exceptional students overuse 'synthetic-global' thinking.

These high-ability and gifted students often have difficulty showing what they know in conventional ways. Not surprisingly, they often lose self-confidence as students, form negative self-efficacy as learners and become disengaged and alienated from the classroom. The research (for example, McCoach and Siegle 2003; Obergriesser and Stoeger 2015; Snyder and Linnenbrink-Garcia 2013) suggests that their underachievement is due to their motivation and emotions. This interpretation, however, is somewhat misleading. At the time of the research mentioned above, the students had already underachieved. It is not, therefore, surprising that they showed negative emotional responses. The emotional and motivational factors were more likely a consequence of earlier underachievement rather than a cause of it.

Psychological issues as second exceptionalities

Some high-ability and gifted students also have psychological issues, such as attention deficit hyperactivity disorder (ADHD) or autism spectrum disorder, or affective disorders, such as oppositional defiant disorder, obsessive compulsive disorder, mood disorders, depression or bipolar (Foley Nicpon et al. 2010). The issue can be due in part to their high learning ability and can also mask their high learning ability.

When twice-exceptional students have ADHD, they show the typical behaviours, such as impulsivity, hyperactivity and distractibility. However, they display them differently from 'regular-learning' ADHD peers (Foley Nicpon et al. 2011). Their intense energy levels, for example, are often more focused and directed rather than random. They may show more intense emotional behaviours and distress, such as mood, anxiety and disruptive behaviour disorders, than either students who have high ability and giftedness or ADHD alone. They may also show more difficult social interactions with peers and their family.

Some high-ability and gifted students also display characteristics linked with autism, such as restricted social and communication skills. These students are on a spectrum, differing in a range of ways. Foley Nicpon et al. (2012) compared the cognitive and academic profiles of high-ability autistic students with and without a delay in language. Autistic students without language delay had higher verbal comprehension, while those with it had better maths fluency and written expression. The *Packet of information for professionals* (PIP) provides a set of recommendations for assisting high-ability and gifted students with autism (Assouline et al. 2008).

Gifted underachievement also sometimes occurs with mood, emotional or 'affective' issues, such as bipolar, depression, paranoia or chronic anxiety and stress. Some studies link the negative emotions with perfectionism. Schools should be aware that this can occur under some conditions for certain students (Grugan et al. 2021; Mofield and Parker Peters 2015).

The learning profiles of twice-exceptional high-ability and gifted students can include aspects of these psychological issues. These aspects need to be considered when supporting these students.

For some high-ability and gifted students, the emotional exceptionality is linked with their approach to learning. They form intuitive theories of action about their social interactions with others, the world and its events just as they form intuitive theories of action in relation to the teaching. They may infer or 'read' negative or threatening consequences in their interactions with peers or others. They may also feel intensely anxious, fearful, paranoid, angry or depressed about world events over which they perceive they have no control.

These students can show a range of debilitating emotions, such as fear and panic, paranoia, extreme anxiety, depression or aggression in response to their theories. Regular students are less likely to generate these inferences and anticipate aspects of their world at this level or to experience the consequential negative emotions.

These issues need to be considered when supporting these students. Educators can infer psychological causes from students' behaviours. There is, however, not a direct mapping between the observed behaviours and the underlying cause. Symptomatic behaviours can overlap with the characteristics of gifted learning. Diagnostic analysis is necessary for the identification of both exceptionalities. Assessment of intellectual, emotional, social and behavioural attributes are needed to investigate whether an individual student is gifted and has psychological issues. These procedures are described in Chapter 6. Advanced understanding, divergent thinking, problem-solving and creativity of these students can vary with their emotional state at any time.

Cultural factors as second exceptionalities

Each student is a member of several cultures, including their family, peer group, racial or ethnic background, gender, community and socioeconomic background. Each culture values particular types of knowledge and ways of doing things. Each student learns and uses this knowledge to interact in these cultures. This is their 'cultural competence' or their 'social and cultural capital'.

All teaching makes assumptions about students' cultural knowledge. Formal education provision also defines high-ability and gifted learning profiles and high-level outcomes from a cultural perspective. As the difference between these assumptions and a student's actual cultural background increases, the opportunities for the student to benefit from the teaching decreases. The increasing interest in the underrepresentation of 'culturally different' students in gifted education provision in the United States reflects this focus (Ford 2010).

The aptitudes, attributes and characteristics associated with high-ability and gifted knowledge are culturally embedded. Students whose cultures value and teach alternative cultural knowledge are sometimes referred to as being from a 'potentially marginalised group', from an 'ethnic minority' culture, or as having a 'diverse cultural and linguistic background'. They are often less likely to have their high-ability and gifted learning profiles recognised and valued in regular classrooms or to have access to teaching that builds on their advanced learning ability (Ford 2010).

It is recommended that teaching and educational provision generally take account of the cultural backgrounds of students. This includes understanding, identifying, valuing and respecting the perspectives on high ability and giftedness held by the students' communities.

Students who are at risk in this way include some First Nations students, students from a diverse cultural and linguistic background, students from a 'low' or 'disadvantaged' socioeconomic background and students from remote or rural areas.

First Nations students

We know that members of Australia's First Nations cultures display high-level outcomes across the gamut of adult pursuits, including in science, art, music, theatre, literature, business and sport. At the same time, First Nations students are underrepresented in high-ability and talent development programs in Australian schools (Thraves and Bannister-Tyrrell 2017). This lack of recognition can be attributed in part to the perspectives of high ability and giftedness used by teachers and schools. These beliefs influence what and how teachers teach, how they interpret students' displays of knowledge, and how they identify and respond to high ability and giftedness. Appropriate provision needs to take account of the perspectives of the relevant First Nations cultures.

The First Nations cultures in Australia differ in how they construct high-ability and gifted knowing and learning (Chandler 2011) and in the ways of knowing and thinking they recognise and value.

A school can initiate dialogue with the local First Nations communities to learn how high ability and giftedness is constructed in those cultures. This can include:

> the types of knowledge that are valued; for example, knowing and understanding in time and space, and how the culture understands and uses science and technology, history or narratives

> how the community thinks; for example, its balance between verbal- and imagery-spatial-mediated thinking, and how the culture frames and solves problems

> the items, activities and events in the culture that can provide a stimulus for high-ability and gifted learning, including collections of art, literature, technology, theatre and environmental and sporting facilities.

The school can also invite a student's parents or carers to discuss how high ability and giftedness is constructed in their family culture. This can include how the family sees the student showing evidence of high-ability and gifted learning. This could be in:

> how the student deals with and solves problems

> the student's interests, drive and what they are intrinsically motivated to do or learn more about

> how the student thinks independently about their world and the types of knowledge they recall most easily

> how the student's knowledge has gradually developed, the developmental pathway they have followed, the aspects of knowledge they seem to have learnt more quickly and how they have adjusted to their world.

This information can inform how typical types of high-ability and gifted profiles can be modified to describe individual students. It can also be used by staff to interpret and resolve issues and challenges that may arise during the student's life in the school.

A reliance on identification procedures that ignore First Nations cultural perspectives and that prioritise 'conventional' assessment protocols, such as standardised achievement tests and intelligence tests, can restrict the opportunity for some First Nations students to display high-ability and gifted profiles or high-level outcomes in the classroom. Tests that are largely verbal or that rely on reading are seen as more biased and less appropriate than non-verbal or spatial–imagery ability tests.

One way of reducing the cultural bias of assessments is to modify the conditions under which the tasks are administered. This can include encouraging and supporting a student to engage with the tasks, removing the need for students to independently read task instructions or breaking the task into smaller steps. The adjusted conditions under which the student can display the assessed skill are then noted. This procedure is called 'dynamic assessment'. It modifies and elaborates conventional identification procedures.

A similar cultural approach can be taken to the development of appropriate teaching and curriculum for high-ability and gifted students from First Nations cultures. This can include the opportunity to explore First Nations culture, language and heritage. First Nations mentors and community Elders can be invited to provide input to the academic program and to be role models. The students can be provided with an opportunity to research their context, culture and history and learn content on Country.

Students from diverse cultural and linguistic backgrounds

High-ability students from language backgrounds other than English may experience challenges when they are required to learn new content in English as their second language and when navigating how to learn in an Australian culture and classroom. Language differences may mean that they think, recall and learn more slowly in English. They may also have different cultural expectations and experiences of school.

The recommendations made for high-ability and gifted underachieving First Nations students are also relevant here.

A school can invite the student's parents or carers to discuss how high ability and giftedness is constructed in the family's culture and can start to build an understanding about the high-ability and gifted student in the culture. This information can be used by staff to describe the individual student's learning profile and to interpret and resolve issues and challenges that arise during the student's life in the school. The identification procedures used by the school, its teaching and curriculum also need to be equitable.

Students from low socioeconomic backgrounds

High-ability students from low socioeconomic backgrounds may also be at risk of underachievement. This could be due to the following:

> Fewer financial resources may mean less opportunity to engage with items, activities and events that can stimulate high-ability and gifted learning. These students may have less access to museums, a range of texts, hobby and leisure involvements in art, theatre, environmental or sporting events.

> There may be fewer opportunities to learn over time because the students need to spend more time in doing everyday chores necessary to support family life.

> Education may be a lower priority for the student's parents or carers than other essential life activities, and the parents or carers may have lower expectations for the student.

> Fewer financial resources may be accompanied by greater ongoing family stress and a lack of physical stability that disrupts and interferes with the student's progress.

The recommendations made for high-ability and gifted underachieving students with other cultural barriers are relevant here. A school can learn from the student's parents or carers how high ability and giftedness is constructed in the family, the resources in the home environment for supporting and stimulating learning and any pressures on the student. This information can inform the student's learning profile and be used to interpret and resolve issues and challenges that arise for the student at school. The earlier comments relating to equitable identification procedures and appropriate teaching and curriculum are also relevant here.

The school can also investigate ways of lowering the potential restricted opportunities for the student. This could include:

> facilitating links with local libraries, museums or other appropriate institutions

> online learning opportunities to supplement classroom learning (including appropriate hardware such as laptops, and wireless internet access via dongles)

> talent development programs run by community organisations, such as music, arts or sporting groups

> parent and carer support groups for these students

> establishing links with mentors.

Students in rural and remote areas

It has already been noted how the development of high-ability and gifted learning profiles and high-level outcomes are facilitated by aspects of a student's environment, the information sources available, items and artefacts in the environment, and the student's involvement in activities and events. Some students live in areas of Australia where these resources are less available. The corresponding features of their environments that might lead to high-level outcomes are often not valued by regular educational provision.

High-ability students in these areas, because of their social isolation, usually have less opportunity to interact with similar-learning peers, less access to high-ability and gifted learning models and less confidence in their knowledge and skills. Their high-level outcomes, relevant to their cultures and environments, may not match those of their peers in the metropolitan areas. They may require a different suite of options for identification and curriculum provision.

Actions schools can take concerning high-ability and gifted underachieving students in remote areas include:

> examining the availability of the resources that support and stimulate learning

> examining how the outcomes of these students match, in quality, those achieved by metropolitan peers

> using identification procedures early in a student's education to recognise possible high ability and giftedness

> investigating opportunities for students to engage in advanced learning through online and virtual classrooms; mentorships and drawing on local expertise in the community; various types of acceleration; and access to learning programs in schools in other locations

> investigating the availability of equity resources to support the student to participate in targeted programs and to overcome geographical isolation

> supporting the student to link with like-minded high-ability and gifted peers and mentors in collaborative learning activities; for example, joint research and projects.

Multiple sources of exceptionality

Some students display multiple sources of exceptionality. A cause in one area may lead to secondary causes in others. For example, a high-ability or gifted student with a specific learning difficulty initially may begin to show behaviours indicative of a psychological exceptionality. Psychological exceptionality can also be a consequence of social isolation, either through remoteness or through cultural or linguistic diversity. These will be indicated in the student's interactions in the classroom and with peers more generally and in how the student responds to everyday life events. The types of assessment described in Chapter 7 will assist in clarifying this. These students will require educational provision that targets their particular exceptionalities, while scaffolding their opportunity to achieve high-level outcomes.

The perplexity of high ability without high-level outcomes

The notion of a high or gifted learning ability without high-level outcomes is perplexing and frustrating for teachers, parents and carers, and the students themselves. They frequently ask: 'How come Student X has been assessed as being gifted but doesn't show it in their outcomes?' This chapter has described several possible reasons for this. For all of the types of twice exceptionality, a student may not achieve high-level outcomes because:

> The classroom context doesn't support them to form intuitive theories of action or scaffold them to convert these to high-level outcomes. This may include the student being unmotivated or believing that their understanding is not valued.

> Classroom teaching and context make assumptions that do not match how the student learns. The teaching doesn't draw on the student's advanced learning capacity and the student may feel disengaged.

> The student's second exceptionality limits their ability to achieve these outcomes.

> The student may be reluctant to show what they know in the classroom. They may feel threatened by thinking differently from their regular learning peers.

When teachers are aware of these possibilities, they can investigate which ones are most pertinent to a particular student and modify the teaching appropriately. They may need to collect relevant information about how the student learns and investigate the conditions under which the student learns best. The content provided in the following chapters addresses this.

What your school can do now

The focus here is on how well teachers in your school understand high-ability and gifted underachievement and what it 'looks like' in regular classrooms. Schools and teachers need to know that a high learning ability doesn't always lead to high-level outcomes.

Some recommended follow-up activities are discussed here.

What does your school know about twice exceptionalities and how to identify them?

Collate what your staff currently know about twice exceptionalities and how to identify them. Some teachers may not be aware of what twice exceptionalities are and what they 'look like' in their classroom. Discuss patterns in the typical outcomes of these students and the indicative behaviours they display in the classroom. Unpack how the apparent inconsistencies in the outcomes and behaviours of these students can be perplexing for teachers and can influence the expectations teachers have for these students.

What are the likely causes of twice exceptionalities?

Discuss the possible causes of the second exceptionality and how it may limit the student's engagement with the teaching. Examine how the second exceptionality can mask the high ability to learn and lead to the student underachieving, disengaging or withdrawing from classroom activities.

Reducing the impact of the second exceptionality often requires its cause to be targeted explicitly. It is useful for teachers to identify possible ways in which this could be done, both within and outside the classroom.

Evaluate the school's current provision for these students

When staff are aware of the twice-exceptional learning profile and its various causes, they are better equipped to evaluate what the school already does in relation to provision for these students and to speculate about how to improve this provision. Staff can identify students who display the characteristics of twice exceptionality, reflect on the conditions under which these students learn best and suggest how, in the future, they might identify and value each student's existing knowledge and ways of learning. Staff can also reflect on how they may restrict the impact of the second exceptionality and scaffold the student to be motivated intrinsically and to build their self-efficacy.

Summary

> Some students with a high-ability or gifted learning profile also have a second learning exceptionality that restricts them from achieving talented outcomes. This can be an academic learning difficulty, a psychological issue, or they may come from a cultural or environmental background that does not match the tacit assumptions made by the teaching.

> These students are 'twice exceptional', 'dual exceptional' or 'gifted underachievers'. Some students have 3 or more exceptionalities.

> The exceptionality can be emotional, social, cultural or cognitive and can lead to academic underachievement, social and behavioural problems and disengagement from regular classroom participation. It can mask the student's high learning capacity and can restrict their ability to achieve high-level outcomes at school.

References

Assouline SG, Foley-Nicpon M and Whiteman C (2010) 'Cognitive and psychosocial characteristics of gifted students with specific learning disabilities', *Gifted Child Quarterly*, 54:102–115, doi:10.1177/001698620935597.

Assouline SG, Nicpon MF, Colangelo N and O'Brien M (2008) *The paradox of giftedness and autism: packet of information for professionals (PIP)* – Revised, Connie Belin & Jacqueline N. Blank International Center for Gifted Education and Talent Development (NJ1).

Beekman TL and Seo HS (2021) 'Analytic versus holistic: cognitive styles can influence consumer response and behavior toward foods', *Journal of Sensory Studies*, e12723, doi:10.1111/joss.12723.

Chandler P (2011) 'Prodigy or problem child? Challenges with identifying Aboriginal giftedness', in Vialle W (ed) *Giftedness from an indigenous perspective*, University of Wollongong, Australian Association for the Education of the Gifted and Talented Ltd., and the Department of Education, Employment and Workplace Relations, Wollongong, accessed 30 October 2023. https://ro.uow.edu.au/uowbooks/16

Foley Nicpon M, Allmon A, Sieck B and Stinson RD (2011) 'Empirical investigation of twice-exceptionality: where have we been and where are we going?', *Gifted Child Quarterly*, 55(1):3–17, doi:10.1177/0016986210382575.

Foley-Nicpon M, Assouline SG and Stinson RD (2012) 'Cognitive and academic distinctions between gifted students with autism and Asperger syndrome', *Gifted Child Quarterly*, 56(2), 77–89, doi:10.1177/0016986211433199.

Foley Nicpon M, Doobay AF and Assouline SG (2010) 'Parent, teacher, and self-perceptions of psychosocial functioning in intellectually gifted children and adolescents with autism spectrum disorder', *Journal of Autism and Developmental Disorders*, 40(8):1028–1038, doi:10.1007/s10803-010-0952-8.

Ford DY (2010) 'Underrepresentation of culturally different students in gifted education: reflections about current problems and recommendations for the future', *Gifted Child Today*, 33(3):31–35.

Gartin BC and Murdick NL (2005) 'Idea 2004: the IEP', *Remedial and Special Education*, 26(6):327–331, doi:10.1177/07419325050260060301.

Grugan MC, Hill AP, Madigan DJ, Donachie T (2021) 'Perfectionism in academically gifted students: a systematic review', *Educational Psychology Review,* 33:1631–1673, doi:10.1007/s10648-021-09597-7.

Institute for the Study of Advanced Development (2019) *Checklist for recognizing twice exceptional children*, Institute for the Study of Advanced Development, Westminster, CO, accessed 27 September. https://static1.squarespace.com/static/5ec9e1a3d3815c7ebcd0503a/t/5fe388beac123c4ebd2795fb/1608747198809/1-20-2019+Checklist+for+Recognizing+2e+Children+%281%29.pdf

Koo M, Choi JA and Choi I (2018) 'Analytic versus holistic cognition: constructs and measurement', in Spencer-Rodgers J and Peng K (eds) *The psychological and cultural foundations of East Asian cognition: contradiction, change, and holism*, Oxford University Press, New York.

Lim L (2021) 'Understanding twice-exceptionality (2e): a multi-systems perspective, *International Journal of Childhood Education*, 2(1):1–11, doi.org/10.33422/ijce.v2i1.34.

McCoach DB and Siegle D (2003) 'Factors that differentiate underachieving gifted students from high-achieving gifted students', *Gifted Child Quarterly*, 47:144–154, doi:10.1177/001698620304700205.

Mofield EL and Parker Peters M (2015) 'The relationship between perfectionism and overexcitabilities in gifted adolescents', *Journal for the Education of the Gifted*, 38(4):405–427, doi:10.1177/0162353215607324.

Munro J (2002) 'Understanding and identifying gifted learning-disabled students', *Australian Journal of Learning Disabilities,* 7:20–30, doi:10.1080/19404150209546698.

Munro J (2005) 'The learning characteristics of gifted literacy disabled students', *Gifted Education International*, 19(2):154–172, doi:10.1177/026142940501900209.

Obergriesser S and Stoeger H (2015) 'The role of emotions, motivation, and learning behavior in underachievement and results of an intervention', *High Ability Studies*, 26(1):167–190, doi:10.1080/13598139.2015.1043003.

Snyder KE and Linnenbrink-Garcia L (2013) 'A developmental, person-centered approach to exploring multiple motivational pathways in gifted underachievement', *Educational Psychologist*, 48:209–228, doi:10.1080/00461520.2013.835597.

Thraves G and Bannister-Tyrrell M (2017) 'Australian Aboriginal peoples and giftedness: a diverse issue in need of a diverse response', *TalentEd*, 29:18–31.

CHAPTER 6

How to identify students who display high-level outcomes

Introduction

So far, we have examined high-ability learning profiles and high-level outcomes in the classroom. We discussed in Chapter 2 how these outcomes are shown on achievement tests and on performance tasks and productions. In Chapter 3 we described the types of understanding that high-ability students form and the thinking and learning personality characteristics they use to form these outcomes. Chapter 4 described the multiple types of high-ability learning profiles and how some are less likely to be recognised in regular teaching.

This chapter focuses on the actions schools can take to identify those students who can display high-level outcomes. It examines the question: Is a student achieving high-level or talented outcomes? Without the appropriate identification tools, some high-ability and gifted students may not be identified. This chapter describes:

> the tasks you can undertake to identify students who form high-level outcomes

> how you can analyse, compare and combine information from several assessment tasks.

The main ideas in this chapter are shown in Figure 6.1.

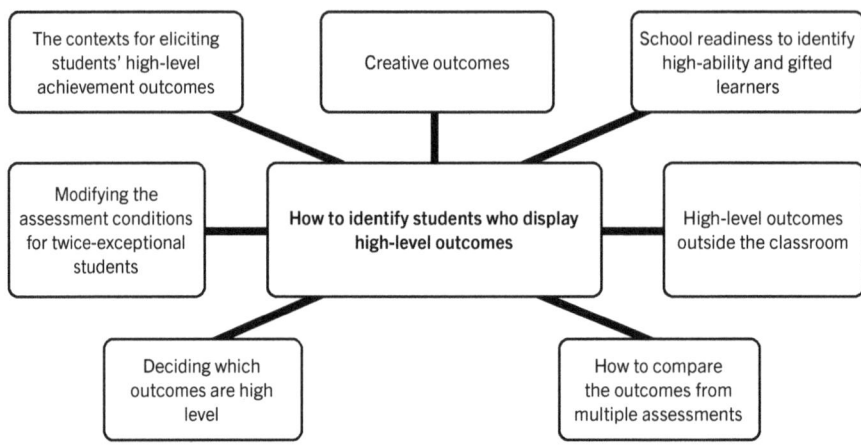

Figure 6.1. How to identify students who display high-level outcomes

How ready is your school to identify high-ability and gifted learners?

Several types of situations can trigger the identification process in relation to high-ability and gifted learners:

> A school wants a systematic set of procedures for identifying high-level outcomes so that it can enhance its educational provision.

> Some students display unexpected high-level achievement on routine group assessments such as tests or productions, either within or outside the educational context.

> Some students form high-level interpretations or intuitive theories of action of the teaching.

> Parents or carers believe that their child has a high learning ability and that the school should target it more explicitly.

Schools and educators need to be ready to respond to these triggers with a systematic identification protocol. Some of the contexts for observing high-level outcomes were introduced in Chapter 2 (see p. 17), including student interpretation of teaching information and student performance in achievement tests and open-ended tasks.

Contexts for eliciting high-level outcomes

Using student responses to teaching

High-ability and gifted students can form interpretations of the teaching that differ from those of their regular learning peers. These interpretations, that is, their intuitive theories of action (ITAs) about the teaching (see Chapters 3 and 4), show evidence of spontaneous inference, analysis and synthesis, contain more ideas than what was in the teaching and lead to more advanced and sophisticated responses in the classroom.

High-ability students can also perceive and respond to more complex challenges and provocations in teaching content and generate more complex questions about it. A framework for embedding more sophisticated provocations in regular teaching that can elicit these more advanced interpretations is described in Chapter 9.

High-ability and gifted students can be invited to share their ITAs about the teaching, which teachers can record and evaluate in terms of the number and quality of the ideas and relationships inferred.

Using teaching to identify instances of high-ability and gifted outcomes is a type of pedagogic identification. Teachers who can, through their formative assessment procedures, recognise these qualities in students' responses, will be more able to identify high-level outcomes in the classroom.

High-ability and gifted students are also more likely to display high-level outcomes when they perceive that the classroom culture and climate support this. This is explored further in Chapter 10, which describes characteristics of cultures that are more conducive to high-ability and gifted students sharing their advanced thinking.

Using achievement tests

As mentioned in Chapter 2, achievement tests can be used to identify high-level and talented outcomes and therefore the students who display them. These tests usually comprise tasks that assess previously taught knowledge or skills in a range of disciplines. The tasks usually differ in their sophistication, complexity or difficulty. The more sophisticated, complex or difficult items are more likely to be answered correctly by the high-ability and talented students.

To be useful for the identification of high-level or talented outcomes, the tasks need to be sufficiently complex, sophisticated or difficult to challenge the high-ability and gifted students, and to separate them from their regular learning peers and other higher ability and gifted students. These tasks spread the scores of more capable learners and allow high-level outcomes to be identified. It is sometimes necessary to use achievement tests that include tasks 2 to 5 year levels above those of high-ability and gifted students' regular peers.

Higher level test items can, for example, ask students to infer implications or possibilities, analyse and evaluate, compare, analogise, generalise or transfer their knowledge. They can require students to retain and manipulate more ideas. A teacher-designed year 3 reading comprehension task can include questions that require comprehension skills or text knowledge typical of years 5 or 6.

Using higher level test items can identify a portion of those students capable of high-level outcomes. These items require students to have the necessary domain knowledge and skill and the ability to display it in the 'window of opportunity' provided by the assessment task. They may, for example, require students to read written tasks and to write their responses. Some high-ability and gifted students, particularly those with the imagery–spatial, performance and twice-exceptional learning profiles, are less able to show high-level or talented outcomes on achievement tests. They may need the assessment conditions to be modified in various ways; for example, the tasks to be read to them, the opportunity to say rather that write their response or to communicate it in other ways.

Achievement test outcomes indicate what a student knows about a predetermined set of ideas or skills. They do not necessarily tell you all the student might know about a topic or how well a person can use a set of skills. For this, you need a more open-ended tool; that is, tasks that are less likely to restrict what a student can share with you.

Using performance or authentic assessment tasks

Performance-based and authentic assessments give students the opportunity to show their knowledge in 'open-ended' tasks, often in response to challenges, from the school curriculum and in real-life contexts. The tasks invite students to show all they know about or can do in relation to a topic and their depth of thinking about it. They provide an alternative window of understanding for students who do not achieve well in or are not motivated to engage with tests. Outcomes from open-ended tasks can supplement students' test outcomes.

Typical tasks include extended written texts, research projects, solving problems, concrete and imagery productions, videotaped recordings, performances or constructions, within and outside the classroom. They include practical achievements in domains such as music, literature, technology, the visual and performing arts, drama or theatre, sports, information technology, computer programming and app development and engineering.

An example of how this sort of task can help uncover students' high-level outcomes is the Type III research tasks in Renzulli's Enrichment Triad Model. Students engage in a broad-based research project in which they actively investigate a real-life problem or issue. The problem or issue has the following characteristics (Reis and Peters 2020; Renzulli 2021):

> ❯ It is personally relevant and of interest to the student and is usually identified or selected by them, sometimes in collaboration with others.

> It is open-ended in the sense that it does not have an established or unique solution from the perspective of the student; as far as they are concerned, it hasn't been solved.

> Its analysis and resolution involves the active use of research and problem-solving skills and information sources and materials that are comparatively advanced for the student's peer group.

> Its resolution has direct implications for aspects of the student's world or members of their community; the outcomes affect 'real' audiences or situations.

Schools can use these types of criteria when designing and implementing performance and authentic assessment tasks.

Schools can also use rubrics to describe the extent to which a student's outcomes differ from those of typical regular peers. The criteria in a rubric can use the characteristics of high-level and talented outcomes described in Chapter 2. Table 6.1 shows a general format for a rubric in which these characteristics have been mapped into criteria. Teachers can use this type of rubric to assess the quality of students' outcomes.

The baseline for applying each criterion in Table 6.1 is a response that is typical of average or regular students. It is allocated a rating of '1'. Outcomes that are more advanced than the baseline for each criterion can be described using the following rating scale: above average responses rated '2', well above average responses rated '3', superior responses rated '4' and exceptional responses rated '5'.

Table 6.1. Rubric for identifying high-level outcomes*

CRITERION The extent to which the outcome:	RATING				
	Average	Above average	Well above average	Superior	Exceptional
achieves a goal or purpose that is advanced or atypical for the cohort	1	2	3	4	5
uses existing knowledge and information in the domain in advanced ways	1	2	3	4	5
shows a broad knowledge of the domain, comprising a wide, advanced range of ideas	1	2	3	4	5
shows a sophisticated depth of understanding of the domain, with ideas analysed, evaluated and linked ideas in advanced, unexpected ways	1	2	3	4	5
shows evidence of curiosity; the ability to question and investigate at a high level	1	2	3	4	5
achieves its intended goal or purpose effectively or functionally, it shows it works at an advanced level	1	2	3	4	5
is creative, original, innovative, novel or unusual	1	2	3	4	5
shows an advanced organisation of its elements; it has clarity, elegance, is aesthetic and shows cohesion	1	2	3	4	5
shows evidence of task commitment and focus, perseverance, intrinsic motivation and the ability to deal with and respond to challenges and barriers that arise	1	2	3	4	5

*A portion of the total score can be allocated to each attribute/criterion and you can use these to calculate a total score for the student. A total average rating score of between 3 and 4 could indicate a high-level outcome and a score of between 4 and 5, a talented outcome.

Each task will assess knowledge and skill in one or more domains. Teachers can modify the criteria to fit the demands of the appropriate domains. Prior to applying a rubric to a particular outcome, teachers can also specify what would constitute evidence for each rating. One way of planning a set of descriptors for a criterion is to ask: What would you expect to be the typical outcome from individuals in the top 5 per cent of the cohort (rating '5' group), the 5 per cent of students just below them (rating '4' group), the 15 per cent of students just below them (rating '3' group), and so on? In other words, what would you expect to be a typical outcome (or descriptor) for each range on the criterion?

This allows you to estimate how typical a learner's behaviours and responses are of their age cohort; for example, how likely it is that the behaviours and responses would be displayed independently and spontaneously by individuals in each range.

Using diffuse problem-solving ability

Some students who have imagery–spatial or practical high-learning ability can show high-level outcomes for a topic more easily by solving open-ended problems (VanTassel-Baska et al. 2007). These are a type of performance or authentic assessment task in which the student is presented with a broad issue or challenge. The problems are open to interpretation or are 'ill-defined'. The task describes a scenario containing an issue and the students need to interpret the scenario as a problem. They also don't have a single solution path. The problems can target either curriculum topics or real-world problems. Diffuse problem-solving is increasingly being used internationally to identify high-ability and gifted students. An example is described in the following scenario.

Scenario: diffuse problem-solving

Great Barrier Reef

> The world's coral reefs are dying because of above average water temperatures. Lord Howe Island has a reef. Parts of it have been badly bleached in recent years, according to Peter Harrison, director of marine studies at Southern Cross University. Warmer than usual waters, light winds and little cloud cover have caused it. 'The warmer water and more light kill the tiny animals that make the corals.'

Schools may need to examine various factors when using problems like the one above as identification tasks. First, the nature of the task may be unfamiliar to some students. They may not be aware of what is expected. Prior to administering the assessment task, it is recommended that students solve 2 or 3 practice problems. For problems typified by the Great Barrier Reef example, they can learn to interpret the diffuse social problem as 'a situation that could be improved/made better' in some way. For each practice example, they can discuss why and how a situation could be improved. They reflect on their role as problem-solvers: how they could 'make the situation better'. Students are guided to apply the following steps to practice problems and receive feedback for their responses to each aspect:

1. Work out what exactly is causing the situation.
2. Imagine what it would look like when it had been 'fixed'.
3. Decide things they might need to know and questions they might ask to know more about it.
4. Think about what they could do to 'fix it.'
5. Imagine what obstacles or barriers could stop them from fixing it or could slow them down.
6. Think about how they could overcome these obstacles.
7. Reflect on how their problem-solving activity could affect others and influence the community.
8. Think about how they could tell if the actions they were taking were actually working.

A second factor schools may need to consider relates to students' existing knowledge of the specific scenario. Students with a better knowledge or experience of the context may be at an advantage over those without. Teachers can take account of this by assessing students' factual knowledge of the context using a pretest. In situations in which the assessment task is administered to a group, the teacher can describe the context to the group or show a video that illustrates the context. This is intended to reduce the likelihood that differences in students' experiential knowledge of the context affect their problem-solving activity.

In earlier work, I describe how this type of open-ended task can be used to identify high-ability and gifted thinking by evaluating students' ability to:

> identify and frame the problem
> describe a possible solution
> compile the steps they would take to solve the problem
> describe the additional information they may need to solve the problem
> identify difficulties and obstacles that may make the problem hard to solve
> infer how they may overcome these difficulties
> identify who may be affected by the problem-solving activity
> infer how they may persuade or convince these people to support their solution
> describe how they could see if their solution was working. (Munro 2015)

Students' responses to each component can be assessed in terms of the quality of the knowledge they display, including:

> the number or fluency of relevant ideas
> the complexity of the thinking that led to it (i.e. literal versus inferential, divergent, far transfer).

The set of responses can also be assessed in terms of its synthesis and cohesion.

Using artificial intelligence to generate authentic assessment tasks

Artificial intelligence platforms can assist teachers to generate open-ended authentic assessment tasks for a topic. By including relevant prompts that refer to the quality of thinking required (for example, critical, analytic, creative, problem-solving), the years of schooling and the depth and breadth of the outcome, teachers can be provided with multiple options. The platforms can also offer possible structures and formats for the outcome, the main components required and the assessment criteria.

It is not recommended that the use of these platforms replace the work of teachers. It is unlikely that a platform can capture the uniqueness and specific focus of a particular classroom. Rather, they can provide options and possibilities that teachers can use to inform their decision-making and modify or adapt to their context.

Is the outcome creative?

The identification of high-ability and gifted learning frequently includes assessing outcomes for creativity (Kaufman and Baer 2006). High-level and talented outcomes often include an element of novelty or creativity. The assessment of authentic performance tasks, for example, includes examining the novelty and originality of outcomes and the thinking that led to them.

Creative outcomes can be categorised in terms of their impact on the culture/s in which they are generated. The 'Four-C Model of Creativity' (Kaufman and Beghetto 2009) identifies creative outcomes that:

> have relevance only to the student who created them ('mini-c' outcomes)

> can be used by a group or culture to achieve a goal in everyday life in a different way ('little-c' outcomes)

> change professional, workplace or vocational practice ('Pro-C' outcomes)

> change how a culture thinks and works ('Big-C' or 'Einstein-level' outcomes).

We usually don't expect school-age students to produce 'Big-C' outcomes, although we know that some past discoveries and innovations had their origin in student thinking and that 'child prodigies' have produced outcomes of this quality.

To identify creative outcomes, schools can use the open-ended performance or authentic assessment tasks described earlier that draw on domain-specific knowledge and skills. The tasks can assess outcomes in a range of contexts, such as everyday events, play, sport, use of language or art activity. The tasks allow original and flexible outcomes. The outcomes can be a product or object, a way of thinking or a set of ideas such as a theory. Students' intuitive theories of action have creative elements.

One context in which students can display creative outcomes is in their response to texts. Texts are used in most domains and can be spoken or written. They include narratives, persuasive and information text and verse, as well as domain-specific texts, such as those used in mathematics, science or information processing (Kaufman et al. 2007). Students can show a high-ability or gifted learning profile in their creative interpretations of texts. Reading comprehension and public speaking formats, such as debating activities, can provide avenues for this. Grigorenko et al. (2008) describe how regular reading comprehension tasks can be modified to elicit creative outcomes.

The creativity of an outcome can be assessed in terms of various criteria, including its:

> novelty or originality, or how unusual or atypical the outcome is for children of that age; this includes novel use of information, ideas and materials

> integration; how well it operates as a 'whole' or has synthesis

> complexity; the breadth or range of ideas the outcome includes, how well it elaborates or reformulates what is known or has been done previously, and the sophistication and complexity in its organisation of ideas

> emotionality; the extent to which the outcome engages its audience by eliciting positive feelings, such as surprise or pleasure – the 'wow' factor

> task appropriateness; how well the outcome achieves its intended purposes or the criteria specified in the task

> elegance; how understandable, elegant, polished, finished or aesthetic the outcome is

> germinality; how well the outcome leads to new perspectives or opportunities or generates new creativity.

The criteria may need to be modified to fit the domain, as they will not necessarily all be equally relevant. Teachers can use the criteria to assess each student's outcome using the rubric presented in Table 6.1 on p. 79. Prior to allocating a rating to a criterion, some teachers prefer to sort or arrange in order a set of outcomes on the criterion. They can then see which outcomes meet the criterion best, next best and so on. They can then decide how outcomes differ on the criterion and use this to allocate the rating.

The assessment of creative outcomes involves a level of subjective judgement. Schools can improve their capacity and confidence in making these assessments using the 'Consensual Assessment Technique' (Baer et al. 2004). Through this process, a panel of experts in a domain develops a set of appropriate criteria and uses these to rate the outcomes of a cohort. It has been used successfully in domains such as art, music, science, mathematics and literature.

Schools can also use existing scales to rate the features of a student's outcome. The 'Creative Product Semantic Scale' uses sets of adjective pairs to assess creative outcomes; for example, 'common–astounding', 'overused–fresh' (O'Quin and Besemer 1989). Each pair of adjectives is on a 7-point Likert scale. Both the Consensual Assessment Technique and the Creative Product Semantic Scale have adequate validity and reliability (Han et al. 2019).

The assessment conditions affect high-level outcomes

The inclusion of this section in a chapter that focuses on identifying students who display high-level outcomes may not be initially obvious to some readers. What is also not obvious, or often overlooked in educational assessment, is the influence of the assessment assumptions or conditions on the likelihood of high-level outcomes.

All the assessment tasks described in this chapter assume particular conditions for obtaining high-level outcomes. These include assumptions about how motivated the students are to engage and their ability to maintain attention, and how well they comprehend the task instructions or know what is expected of them. Some students might display high-level outcomes on achievement tests or on performance and authentic tasks when the tasks are presented in alternative ways and under other assessment conditions. Some, for example, have difficulty reading instructions and responding by writing. The assessment may need to be 'in situ' and allow a student to show their understanding by speaking, making a video or a model or showing their understanding in other multimodal assessment formats.

These are the twice-exceptional students described in Chapter 5. They are more able to display high-level outcomes when the assessment conditions and assumptions are modified to take account of their learning profiles.

There are 2 directions educators can take here. They can accept the outcome displayed in the given assessment context and ignore the possibility of context influences. Or, they can acknowledge this possibility by giving students the opportunity to respond to these tasks under alternative conditions. Educators can provide this opportunity when they have other evidence that suggests that a student can display high-level outcomes; for example, they have done so in their past.

High-level outcomes outside the classroom

As noted earlier some students display high-level knowledge and skills of the world or practical problem-solving in contexts outside the classroom. These include practical achievements in domains such as music, literature, technology, the visual and performing arts such as dance or sculpture, drama or theatre, sports, information technology, app development or engineering.

These outcomes have often been initiated by the individual student's interests and achieved through their self-directed learning activity, intrinsic motivation, task commitment and determination. They are evidence of what this student can achieve.

Some schools ignore or disregard these outcomes. They lack procedures for collecting and interpreting information about them. This book believes that these outcomes are relevant to interpreting the student's areas of high-ability and talented achievements. Schools can invite external experts in the area of achievement to evaluate the outcomes in terms of their quality and how typical they are of the student's age range. An outcome could be rated as:

> - exceptional (very few students display this level of achievement)
> - very high
> - above average
> - average
> - below average.

Parents, carers and peers often observe students achieving these advanced outcomes and can comment on current or past achievements. Parent/carer, peer and self-rating scales are useful here. For parents, these can include developmental milestones in cognition, language, emotional and social maturity, and motor perceptual development. Students can also provide self-ratings as to how they perceive their achievements.

Deciding which outcomes are high level

To decide which outcomes for a cohort are high level or talented, we need to take account of several points:

> - Student outcomes on achievement tasks (tests and authentic performance tasks) are usually allocated scores that are 'approximately normally distributed'. Educators use the normal distribution to help answer the question: How far is a student's outcome above the average for the

cohort? The normal distribution shows where the student is located relative to peers in a 'standard' cohort. This is their 'percentile rank'. It also shows how many standard deviations above the average a student's score is. This is their 'z-score'. High-level outcomes are those that have the highest scores.

> There is a lack of consistency in the criteria used to identify the cut-off score selected for a high-level outcome (Harding et al. 2018:5). Some educators and researchers select the top 10 per cent of outcomes as talented, some the top 5 per cent and some the top 2 or 1 per cent of scores.

> Some educators and researchers select score ranges that are either one or 2 standard deviations above the average as talented.

This book uses Gagné's (2020) 'metric-based' system for describing high-level and talented outcomes and comprises:

> high achievers in the 75th–89th percentile range

> talented outcomes in the 90th–99th percentile range

> highly talented outcomes in the 99th–99.8th percentile range

> exceptionally talented outcomes in 99.9th–99.98th percentile range

> extremely or profoundly talented outcomes in the 99.99th–99.999th percentile range.

To see whether a student's outcomes are in the top 15 to 25 per cent of outcomes, you can convert their scores on the tasks you have used to percentile rank scores. For standardised normed achievement tests, most test manuals will tell you directly the percentile rank that matches a particular raw score for the appropriate age or year range.

For teacher-designed tests and for other tasks, the students' raw scores for each task need to be converted to percentile ranks. You may have colleagues who can use Excel to do this and there are short online tutorials that explain the process. You can also search for 'raw score to percentile conversion' and similar online.

You want to know the raw scores in the data set that match the 75th, 90th and 99th percentile. When you know the percentile rank that matches each raw score, you can work out the range of raw scores that go from the 75th to 89th percentiles. This is the 'high achievers' range. You can also see the range of raw scores that go from the 90th to 99.999th percentiles. This is the 'talented outcomes' range. If you have enough test items and enough students, you may be able to see the range of raw scores that go from the 99th to 99.999th percentiles (the highly talented outcomes).

How to compare outcomes from multiple assessments

It is generally understood that decisions about whether a student displays high-level outcomes are more valid and accurate when information from multiple tasks is compared or combined. You can compare a student's percentile rank scores on various tasks and note whether each score falls in the average, high achiever, or talented outcome ranges. From this, you can identify the conditions under which a particular student can form these outcomes. The information collected from various sources could be collated in a format similar to that shown in Table 6.2.

Table 6.2. Comparing outcomes from multiple assessments

ASSESSMENT	NAME OF TASK	DATE(S) OF ASSESSMENT	PERCENTILE RANK
Standard academic achievement tests			
Teacher-prepared achievement tests			
Performance or authentic assessment tasks			
Creativity tasks			
Teacher observation or rating			
Parent/carer rating			
Peer rating			
Self-rating by learners			

What your school can do now

To implement provision for high-ability and gifted students, schools need equitable, valid and reliable procedures for identifying and interpreting high-level outcomes. These can be identified in several ways. Some recommended follow-up activities are given here.

Review assessment procedures

Review the assessment procedures and tools your school currently uses in terms of their adequacy for identifying a range of high-level outcomes. You can use this content to create a set of criteria to evaluate the current provision. This can include:

> the types and breadth of tasks used

> the extent to which higher level knowledge and understanding is assessed

> the extent to which the tasks assess creativity and innovation.

Plan tasks that identify high-level outcomes

Have teachers plan achievement tests and authentic performance tasks that will identify high-level outcomes for topics they will teach. Teachers can plan:

> achievement tests that assess higher level knowledge and understanding

> authentic performance tasks

> diffuse problem-solving tasks.

Establish data interpretation abilities

Identify teachers' ability to interpret student outcome data. The school needs procedures for interpreting students' scores on outcomes and selecting those that are high level. Teachers can benefit from knowing how to apply these procedures; for example, knowing how to convert raw scores on teacher-developed tasks and open-ended assessments to percentile ranks. It is also useful for them to know how to compare and interpret scores from multiple achievements tasks. Workshops to teach data interpretation and how to select students who display high-level outcomes may be necessary.

Evaluate your school's current provision

After you have reviewed the assessment procedures that your school currently uses, invite staff to recommend ways in which the school's procedures and tools could be improved. You can create a set of criteria for 'ideal' identification practice and use it to evaluate the school's current provision and to identify ways in which it could be improved. The perceptions of students and parents and carers could also inform this evaluation.

Summary

> - One indicator of high learning ability is high-level achievement. Schools can identify high-level outcomes using achievement tests and open-ended performance and authentic assessment tasks. The open-ended tasks, including complex problem-solving tasks, are useful with students whose high learning ability is in the imagery–spatial or practical domains.
>
> - The identification of high-ability and gifted learning frequently includes assessing outcomes for creativity.
>
> - The assessment conditions can be modified for twice-exceptional students.

> High-level outcomes outside the classroom can contribute to interpreting the student's learning profile.

> Gagné's (2020) 'metric-based' system can be used to describe high-level and talented outcomes.

> For teacher-designed tests and tasks, students' raw scores on each task need to be converted to percentile ranks. Percentile ranks can be used to compare the outcomes from multiple assessments.

References

Baer J, Kaufman JC and Gentile CA (2004) 'Extension of the consensual assessment technique to nonparallel creative products', *Creativity Research Journal*, 16(1):113–117, doi:10.1207/s15326934crj1601_11.

Gagné F (2020) *Differentiating giftedness from talent: the DMGT perspective on talent development*, Routledge, New York, doi:10.4324/9781003088790.

Grigorenko EL, Jarvin L, Tan M and Sternberg RJ (2008) 'Something new in the garden: assessing creativity in academic domains', *Psychology Science*, 50(2):295–307.

Han J, Hua M, Shi F and Childs PR (2019) 'A further exploration of the three driven approaches to combinational creativity', in *Proceedings of the design society: international conference on engineering design* (Vol. 1, No. 1), Cambridge University Press.

Harding SM, English N, Nibali N, Griffin P, Graham L, Alom B and Zhang Z (2019) 'Self-regulated learning as a predictor of mathematics and reading performance: a picture of students in grades 5 to 8', *Australian Journal of Education*, 63(1):74–97: doi:10.1177/0004944119830153.

Institute for the Study of Advanced Development (2019) *Checklist for recognizing twice exceptional children*, Institute for the Study of Advanced Development, Westminster, CO, accessed 27 September 2023. https://static1.squarespace.com/static/5ec9e1a3d3815c7ebcd0503a/t/5fe388beac123c4ebd2795fb/1608747198809/1-20-2019+Checklist+for+Recognizing+2e+Children+%281%29.pdf

Kaufman JC and Baer J (2006) 'Intelligent testing with Torrance', *Creativity Research Journal*, 18(1):99–102.

Kaufman JC and Beghetto RA (2009) 'Beyond big and little: the four-c model of creativity', *Review of General Psychology*, 13(1):1–12, doi:10.1037/a0013688.

Kaufman JC, Lee J, Baer J and Lee S (2007) 'Captions, consistency, creativity, and the consensual assessment technique: new evidence of reliability', *Thinking skills and creativity*, 2(2):96–106, doi:10.1016/j.tsc.2007.04.002.

Munro JK (2015) 'Scenario problem solving: a measure of the quality of gifted students' thinking', *Australasian Journal of Gifted Education*, 24(1):23–29.

O'Quin K and Besemer SP (1989) 'The development, reliability, and validity of the revised creative product semantic scale', *Creativity Research Journal*, 2(4):267–278, doi:10.1080/10400418909534323.

Reis SM and Peters P (2020) 'Research on the Schoolwide Enrichment Model: four decades of insights, innovation, and evolution', *Gifted Education International*, 37(2):109–141, doi:10.1177%2F0261429420963987.

Renzulli JS (2021) 'Anatomy of a type III enrichment project', *Renzulli Center for Creativity, Gifted Education, and Talent Development*, University of Connecticut, Connecticut, accessed 14 March 2024. https://gifted.uconn.edu/wp-content/uploads/sites/961/2022/05/Anatomy-of-a-Type-III-Enrichment-Project.pdf.

VanTassel-Baska J, Feng AX and De Brux E (2007) 'A study of identification and achievement profiles of performance task-identified gifted students over 6 years', *Journal for the Education of the Gifted*, 31(1):7–34, doi:10.4219/jeg-2007-517.

CHAPTER 7

Does a student have a high-ability and gifted learning profile?

Introduction

Chapter 6 described how schools can identify high-level outcomes. We've already noted that some students who have the capacity to form these outcomes don't necessarily do so. In this chapter, we examine how a school can identify each type of high-ability learning profile. The tasks described here assess the extent to which students show the types of profiles and learning characteristics described in Chapter 4. They allow you to detect those students who could achieve high-level outcomes but don't. It also provides useful information for planning effective provision for high-ability and gifted students.

The model of learning used in this book proposes that high-ability or gifted learning profiles lead to high-level and talented outcomes respectively. To understand and identify both the learning profiles and the outcomes, we need observable responses from students.

To infer the learning profiles, we need to monitor and evaluate students' learning activities that lead to these outcomes. This includes being able to observe and collect evidence of the thinking skills students use, the ways in which they link ideas and the learning behaviours indicative of their intrinsic motivation, their curiosity and their task commitment.

This chapter focuses on identifying student behaviours and responses indicative of high-ability and gifted learning profiles. From the perspective of the model of learning used in this book, the observable skills, behaviours and responses examined in this chapter are not categorised as outcomes.

You can identify behaviours indicative of a high-ability and gifted profile by using a range of teaching tasks in multiple contexts. These tasks identify advanced understanding, knowledge or skill; advanced capacity to infer, analyse, synthesise, relate and think creatively; and students' motivation to learn, intrinsically and extrinsically. They also involve making comparisons with a student's peers and can facilitate the identification of students who could achieve high-level outcomes but don't.

The main ideas in this chapter are shown in Figure 7.1.

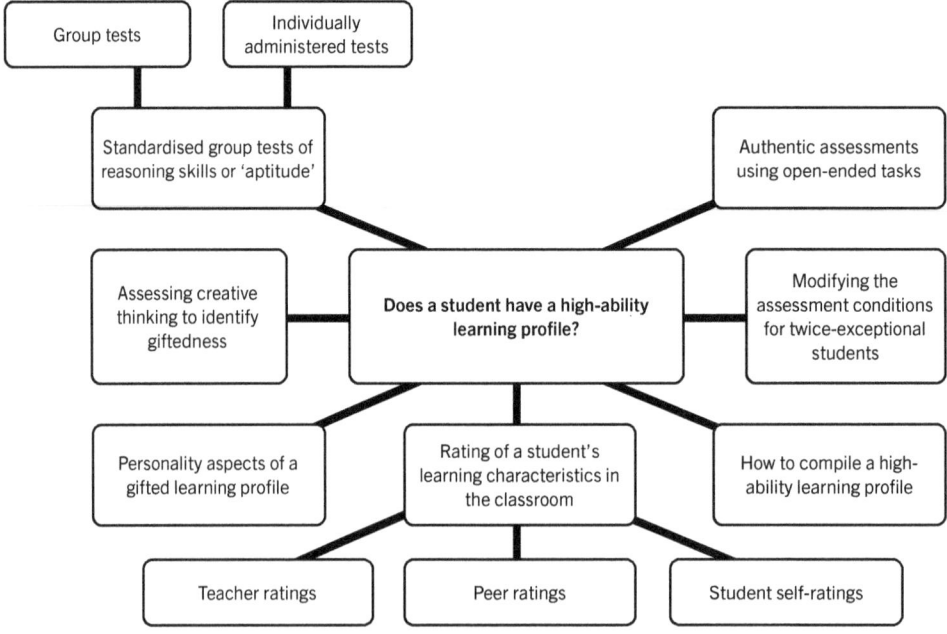

Figure 7.1. Does a student have a high-ability and gifted learning profile?

Standardised tests of reasoning skills or 'aptitude'

Standardised or normed tests of knowledge and reasoning skills are used to describe a student's learning potential, general ability, intelligence or aptitude. Both group and individually administered assessments are available.

Group tests of reasoning skills or aptitude

These tests are intended to assess how well students use specific thinking or reasoning skills in verbal, quantitative, abstract, action and spatial domains. They include short answer and multiple-choice tests given to a group of students at a particular time, administered either on paper or online. The types of tasks assess:

> vocabulary, by recognising synonyms and antonyms for a given word

> verbal analogising

> reasoning about symbolic and abstract patterns

> manipulating spatial and figural patterns

> quantitative patterns.

There is a wide range of aptitude tests available. Table 7.1 includes examples and shows what each tell you and their intended age or year range. They differ in how they estimate overall general ability, intelligence, potential, aptitude or reasoning ability in specific domains.

Table 7.1. Group tests of reasoning or aptitude

TEST	ABILITY REPORTED	INTENDED RANGE
ACER General Ability Tests (AGAT) (ACER 2023a)	Reasoning skills in 2 or more domains	Years 2 to 11
Higher Ability Selection Test (HAST) (ACER 2023b)	Scores are combined to estimate general ability	Years 5 to 11

Table 7.1 continued

Raven's Standard Progressive Matrices (SPM) (Raven 1992)	Spatial reasoning skills Scores estimate fluid or non-verbal ability	Ages 5 to 18+
Cognitive Abilities Test (CogAT) (Lakin 28 January 2019)	Verbal, quantitative and non-verbal (spatial) reasoning domains, ability for each domain and a general ability	Prep to Year 12

The group tests of reasoning provide a broad assessment of students' reasoning skills and are usually used for screening purposes. This is often the first step in identifying high-ability and gifted learning profiles in a group of students.

They report students' reasoning ability using standard scores and percentile ranks. They assess these skills reliably and validly. It is recommended that you use percentile rank scores to see which students use thinking in the high-ability and gifted ranges. By comparing a student's scores on each of the domains, you can see the domain(s) in which students show either high-ability or gifted learning profiles.

It should be remembered that the test scores are not totally precise. Each test has an 'inaccuracy factor' that is indicated by its 'standard error of measurement'. This gives an indication of how confident you can be in a student's score.

These inaccuracies are affected by the assumptions made by the test. The tests usually assume that students can read and comprehend tasks independently, that they can maintain on-task attention and focus and that they are motivated to complete the test. These factors need to be taken into account when interpreting scores.

The format shown in Table 7.1 can be used by schools to collate and organise the specific tests they use. It helps to ensure that the school's test collection adequately covers the range of knowledge and skills. It also assists in selecting appropriate tests.

Some schools use external assessment agencies. To interpret and use the scores they provide, it is useful to know the reasoning skills assessed by each test and to use percentile rank scores on the tests to interpret their outcomes.

Individually administered tests of general ability or aptitude

High-ability and gifted learning profiles can also be identified using individually administered scales. These scales usually assess a broader range of reasoning skills using a more comprehensive range of assessment tasks and offer a more in-depth description of students learning profiles.

Examples of individually administered tests are the Wechsler Intelligence Scale for Children V (WISC V; Wechsler 2014) and the Stanford Binet Intelligence Test (Fifth Edition) (SB5; Roid and Pomplun 2012). Each of these scales measures multiple areas of reasoning. The WISC-V, for example, assesses verbal comprehension, visual spatial reasoning, fluid reasoning, working memory and processing speed. Each area has at least 2 sub-tests. A student can have high ability and giftedness in one or more of verbal comprehension, visual or spatial reasoning and fluid reasoning and differences between these areas can help you identify a student's learning profile. One student may be gifted in verbal comprehension, while a second may be gifted in visual–spatial reasoning. Individually administered tests also assist in identifying culturally diverse and twice-exceptional students.

Individually administered test scales differ in the tasks they include and differ in who they identify as gifted. The WISC-V has more tasks that assess abstract verbal reasoning and identifies more highly verbal children, while the SB5 is likely to find more mathematically and spatially gifted children.

Administering an assessment individually can reduce or remove some of the factors that restrict the accuracy of the group administered tests. First, students do not need to read and comprehend tasks independently; the examiner presents the tasks orally. Second, the examiner can scaffold the student to focus and maintain on-task attention. Third, the examiner can provide extrinsic motivation when the student's intrinsic motivation seems to fall. Fourth, the examiner can match the tasks presented to a student's performance pattern; presentation of the tasks in an area usually stops after the student provides a specified number of incorrect responses. The extent of external control provided by the examiner here has led some educators to suggest that the individually administered assessments provide a more accurate assessment of high ability and giftedness than the group assessments (Rimm et al. 2008).

The individually administered tests are frequently used following the use of group tests. Once a student has been identified as having a high-ability or gifted learning profile using a group test, the individual assessments offer a more detailed and elaborated description of the profile. The use of individual assessments such as the WISC-V and the SB5 is restricted to qualified professionals such as psychologists. Your school may receive reports of students' outcomes on these assessments. It is useful for staff to be able to interpret them in terms of the students' learning profiles and to identify their implications for educational provision.

Authentic assessments using open-ended tasks

Standardised general ability or aptitude tests that require students to read instructions or task descriptions identify a restricted range of high-ability and gifted students. They are more likely to exclude those whose high learning ability is in the non-verbal, procedural, practical or twice-exceptional categories. Students with these profiles are more likely to be identified using authentic assessment formats.

Authentic and performance tasks can provide the opportunity for students to generate high-ability and talented outcomes, as described in Chapter 6. These assessment tasks (see p. 77) also provide the opportunity for students to show or 'do' their high-ability and gifted understanding and thinking, as well as their intrinsic motivation, drive, commitment and perseverance, more independently in an integrated way, in 'real life' and the classroom.

These tasks ask students to use 'big picture' thinking about complex relationships in an interdisciplinary way. The performance high-ability and gifted scenarios described earlier for Siddarth and Rory (see Chapter 4, pp. 46–47) are examples of how practically gifted students can display their learning capacity in this way.

Students' learning and thinking activity can be recorded in portfolios over an extended period and evaluated for evidence of higher level understanding, thinking, creativity, task commitment and focus. Students can use these tasks to 'tell the story' of their high-ability and gifted understanding of the issue and to show their gifted knowing and thinking. The information collected can be assessed for evidence of high-ability and gifted profiles and can supplement students' test outcomes. It provides an alternative window for displaying high-level or gifted learning ability for students who do not achieve well in tests or who haven't been motivated to demonstrate their talent via other standard indicators.

Schools that intend to use open-ended tasks to identify high-ability and gifted students need to provide the appropriate conditions for collecting evidence of students' learning activity. Task completion may involve students using a range of skills. They may need time to unpack the goal or focus, develop an overall plan and implement it in a self-directed way, dealing with unexpected factors that arise.

Using authentic tasks to identify high-ability and gifted learning profiles

Students' activity as they progress through performance or authentic assessment tasks can be monitored and scored in terms of the extent to which it aligns with high-ability and gifted learning profiles. A rubric for doing this can be used. It can be generated using the characteristics of high-ability and gifted learning described in Chapter 3. This information can be collected in various ways:

> Students can maintain a journal in which they record how they work through a task, their reflections on their thinking and their change in understanding.

> Teachers can plan how they will observe, record and interpret student learning activity in an ongoing way.

> Teachers can schedule periodic meetings with the student to discuss and review relevant aspects of their progress.

A set of generic rubrics for any topic is presented in Tables 7.2a to 7.2f. Each table's caption describes a dimension that indicates the quality or complexity of the criterion included. A student's learning activity is rated on each criterion, in comparison with the student's cohort, as follows: well below average activity is rated 1, below average activity is rated 2, average activity is rated 3, above average activity is rated 4 and well above average activity is rated 5. The specific characteristics of each rating will depend on the domain being assessed.

Teachers can use these criteria to guide their collection of information about the student's learning activity and to score it.

Table 7.2. Rubrics for scoring authentic assessment tasks
a. Quality of interpretation of the task and the goal or purpose of the outcome

CRITERION	RATING				
Evidence that the student shows advanced skill in interpreting the task independently and framing up a goal or purpose that is:	Well below average	Below average	Average	Above average	Well above average
clear, well defined and appropriate	1	2	3	4	5
creative and innovative	1	2	3	4	5
appropriate for the intended audience	1	2	3	4	5

b. Quality of domain knowledge

CRITERION	RATING				
Evidence that the student's domain knowledge:	Well below average	Below average	Average	Above average	Well above average
is advanced in its breadth or comprehensiveness	1	2	3	4	5
is advanced in its depth	1	2	3	4	5
is organised logically with key ideas linked	1	2	3	4	5
includes creative, original ideas and interpretations	1	2	3	4	5
includes 'big' ideas	1	2	3	4	5

c. Ability to think at a high level

CRITERION	RATING				
Evidence that the student:	Well below average	Below average	Average	Above average	Well above average
analyses, evaluates and compares ideas in advanced ways	1	2	3	4	5
infers possibilities, makes analogies	1	2	3	4	5
applies ideas in novel, unexpected ways	1	2	3	4	5
integrates and synthesises ideas, generates 'big' ideas	1	2	3	4	5
thinks creatively and divergently	1	2	3	4	5
can retain and think about a comparatively high number of ideas at once	1	2	3	4	5
solves problems in unusual, novel or innovative ways, asks complex questions about ideas	1	2	3	4	5
uses imagination or fantasy and often shows 'intellectual playfulness'	1	2	3	4	5
uses action sequences in innovative ways	1	2	3	4	5
uses these thinking strategies independently and selectively	1	2	3	4	5

d. Ability to monitor and self-regulate thinking

CRITERION	RATING				
Evidence that the student:	Well below average	Below average	Average	Above average	Well above average
develops independently an exceptional plan to achieve the outcome	1	2	3	4	5
implements their plan, monitors their progress and modifies their plan where necessary	1	2	3	4	5
reviews their emerging understanding and activity	1	2	3	4	5
responds to challenges and barriers that arise	1	2	3	4	5
reflects on their overall learning activity and is prepared to modify it	1	2	3	4	5

Table 7.2. continued

e. Ability to select, organise and use relevant information

CRITERION	RATING				
Evidence that the student:	Well below average	Below average	Average	Above average	Well above average
selects and uses in advanced ways information sources, references and resource materials that are appropriate to the task	1	2	3	4	5
uses advanced, technical or complex resource materials or equipment	1	2	3	4	5
uses a comparatively diverse range of resource materials	1	2	3	4	5

f. Quality of emotional engagement with the task

CRITERION	RATING				
Evidence that the student:	Well below average	Below average	Average	Above average	Well above average
shows focused, intense interest in the topic	1	2	3	4	5
shows enthusiasm and curiosity	1	2	3	4	5
is self-motivated to think and learn about the topic and shows high academic intrinsic motivation and a drive to learn more	1	2	3	4	5
has a high self-concept and self-efficacy	1	2	3	4	5
shows task commitment, focus, endurance and persistence and is prepared to commit time, effort and energy	1	2	3	4	5
shows personal standards of intellectual activity and creativity	1	2	3	4	5

You can design authentic assessment tasks for any topic you teach and include a rubric to identify high-ability and gifted learning. Domains can differ in the criteria they require in a rubric and how teachers interpret them.

The efficacy of your rubric relies on how well you can describe a student's outcome on each criterion. You can moderate your judgement by having colleagues also rate the outcomes and compare and justify your ratings.

Assess creative thinking to identify giftedness

Chapter 6 noted that high-level outcomes usually include an element of novelty. This element requires the ability and motivation to think creatively and is referred to in high-ability and gifted learning profiles as the student's 'creative potential'. As well as assessing the creative quality of a student's outcomes, schools can assess a student's creative thinking ability.

Tests of creative potential assess specific cognitive processes such as thinking divergently, making associations, constructing and combining broad categories or working on many ideas simultaneously. These tests have not been used widely to identify high-ability and gifted students in Australia. These tests include the Torrance Tests of Creative Thinking (TTCT) (Torrance 1999), the Remote Associates Test (RAT) (Mednick 1962), Alternate Uses (Wallach and Kogan 1965), the Test of Creative Thinking (TCT-DP) (Urban and Jellen 1996) and the Evaluation of Potential Creativity (Lubart et al. 2011).

The tasks generally assess the ability to think creatively about verbal and figural scenarios. Outcomes are scored in terms of their:

> fluency; the breadth of knowledge, using the number of responses to the specified tasks

> flexibility of thinking; the breadth of thinking displayed, the ability to think creatively and divergently make novel associations and the ability to analyse, evaluate and synthesise

> originality; the 'uncommonness' or uniqueness of the outcomes

> elaboration; the quality of the links or associations made between ideas, and how divergent the links are

> resistance to premature closure; how prepared the individual is to continue to investigate possibilities

> usefulness; how practical and relevant the outcomes are.

In a reanalysis of Torrance's (1972) elementary school longitudinal study, Plucker (1999) notes that verbal creativity scores on the Torrance Tests predicted creative achievements better than IQ scores assessment when the students became adults 20 years later. Evaluations of how well other tests of creative potential work can be found in reviews by Barbot et al. (2011) and Cropley (2000).

Modifying assessment conditions for twice-exceptional students

Chapter 6 noted how the assessment context may need to be modified to allow twice-exceptional students to show high-level outcomes. Contexts can be similarly modified to help these students show aspects of their learning profiles.

We make these modifications using 'dynamic assessment procedures'. Teachers can also use dynamic assessment to identify whether a student uses high-level thinking when the assessment conditions are changed. This may include modifying the format, providing more practice or scaffolding particular ways of thinking about the tasks. Lidz and Macrine (2001) describe how teachers can use the procedure.

Chapter 5 noted how some gifted students have difficulty learning literacy conventions, how to spell or how to write effectively. This may prompt teachers to ask, 'How can a student be gifted but not spell or write well?' Learning literacy skills involves thinking in analytic sequential ways about letter–sound patterns (that is, phonemic processing) and being programmed externally. Many gifted students use global thinking more than analytic sequential thinking and are self-programming.

For highly able students who have literacy difficulties, instructions can be given orally rather than through reading. They can show their understanding in alternative formats; they can say it, show it in a video or a model or in other multimodal formats. You can also modify the task conditions for students who are disengaged or who have emotional issues. This can include modifying or shortening the length of time the student spends on their task at any sitting, providing additional practice examples, personalising the task and helping them see the progress they are making. Similarly, the conditions may need to be modified for students who are from diverse linguistic or cultural backgrounds. Again, the assumptions made by the regular assessment tasks need to be adjusted to take account of differences.

It is useful for a school to have diagnostic information about the area of exceptionality that restricts the student's ability to achieve high-level outcomes. These include the student's reading and writing ability, emotional and social challenges, their motivation to engage and their ability to comprehend the task instructions or know what is expected of them. This information can assist in selecting the most appropriate conditions for obtaining outcomes.

Rating a student's learning characteristics

Teachers and peers observe instances of a student's knowledge, thinking, approach to learning, interest and problem-solving ability in the classroom. Parents observe corresponding instances in contexts beyond the classroom and are witness to their children's perceptions of their classroom experiences. Ratings from teachers, peers, parents and the students themselves provide useful information for informing the identification of high-ability and gifted learning profiles (Lee and Olszewski-Kubilius 2006; Worrell and Erwin 2011).

Teachers rating learning characteristics

Teachers can describe students' approach to learning on a range of criteria to help identify those who have a high-learning ability; for example:

> how they think and learn

> their emotional engagement with the learning activity (their 'learning personality', including their intrinsic motivation to learn, spontaneous enquiry, self-regulation, persistence in completing tasks and independence of learning)

> their display of intuitive theories of action, creative outcomes, evidence of lateral thinking and production of creative outcomes.

The observational checklist shown in Table 7.3 is an example of how teachers might rate a student's learning characteristics. The 5-point rating scale ranges from rarely (1) to very often (5).

Table 7.3. Observational checklist for rating learning characteristics

LEARNING CHARACTERISTICS How often while learning a topic does the student:	RATING				
	Rarely	Occasionally	Sometimes	Fairly often	Very often
show high understanding, rather than low-level interpretation or application?	1	2	3	4	5
link ideas in lateral, broad unexpected ways?	1	2	3	4	5
keep track of several ideas at once and think in several directions?	1	2	3	4	5
think in larger jumps and skip steps in their thinking?	1	2	3	4	5
quickly see novel connections between ideas or infer?	1	2	3	4	5
solve problems in unusual or novel ways?	1	2	3	4	5
spontaneously ask complex questions about ideas?	1	2	3	4	5
use imagination or fantasy or show 'intellectual playfulness'?	1	2	3	4	5
show focused, intense interest in a topic?	1	2	3	4	5
show self-motivation to think and learn about the topic?	1	2	3	4	5

differ in how easily they spontaneously and selectively use the above ways of thinking?	1	2	3	4	5
monitor and direct their learning independently; review progress?	1	2	3	4	5
extend the teaching spontaneously by inferring patterns, rules and relationships?	1	2	3	4	5

Students whose average rating is in the 4 to 5 range are more likely to have a high-ability or a gifted learning profile.

Commercial rating scales for observing these learning behaviors objectively for the K–Year 12 range include:

> Scales for Identifying Gifted Students (SIGS) (Ryser and McConnell 2004)

> Gifted Evaluation Scales (GES-3) (McCarney and Arthaud 2009)

> Scales for Rating the Behavioral Characteristics of Superior Students (Renzulli et al. 2002)

> Universal Talented and Gifted Screener (McCallum and Bracken 2018).

These scales have reliability and validity. Some also include ratings of high-level outcomes in specific domains, such as English or mathematics.

Another tool is the Purdue Academic Rating Scales (PARS) (Feldhusen et al. 1990) that secondary teachers can use to identify high-ability and gifted student learning behaviours in English, mathematics, science, social studies and foreign languages (it can also be used with primary-level students). A score can be calculated for each domain and averaged across the domains, indicating the extent to which a student's high-ability and gifted thinking is generalised across subject areas.

Peer ratings of a student's ability to learn

A student's peers can describe what they observe about how the student knows, understands and learns. Responses can be elicited via questionnaires that ask peers to rate the student's:

> approach to learning

> achievement

> confidence and competence as a learner and a leader

> interpersonal and social skills, flexibility in social interactions

> goal aspirations.

Peer nomination has various limitations. Some peers may use inappropriate criteria; for example, friendship. Some may not 'see' the high ability or giftedness in their peers. Peer referrals have fair-to-adequate reliability and limited evidence of validity (Worrell and Erwin 2011). You can use them when the peers have had sufficient time to know the student and when they know the purpose of the peer-nomination activity.

Student self-perceptions and ratings

Most high-ability and gifted students know what they know, how they learn and think and their feelings and dispositions to learning. You can give them the opportunity to 'tell their gifted story' in contexts within and beyond the classroom. They decide what they want to tell you. They can describe their interests, their knowledge of topics in which they are interested and how they learn and think. A useful procedure for gathering the information is to ask the students to respond to the following open-ended questions (Bakx et al. 2021):

> What do I like to do?

> How am I?

> What are my characteristics?

> What can I do well?

> What can't I do well?

High-performing students are more likely to describe personal characteristics and skills, while regular students refer to achievements in particular areas, for example, sport (Bakx et al. 2021).

Information from parents or guardians

Parents see their children's achievements and ways of thinking outside of the educational setting. This information can enhance the perceptions of educators and peers. It can be collected in various ways; for example, parents can:

> write or audio-record a description that 'tells the gifted story' of their child and that refers to as many 'concrete' instances as possible

> complete questionnaires that guide them to reflect on and report their child's thinking and learning.

Parent questionnaires ask about the child's:

> learning characteristics and interest in everyday activities; for example, whether the child is highly curious, learns rapidly, teaches themselves and recalls quickly what they've learned or initiates investigating topics that interest them

> vocabulary and general knowledge of the world

> imagination and sense of humour

> developmental history and when they acquired developmental milestones, such as beginning to move and walk, talk, read, write or use numbers

> self-directed pursuits and interests and areas of high-level achievement outside school

> attitudes to school and learning in the classroom

> social interaction skills, social maturity and quality of peer social relationships

> everyday problem-solving skills, resourcefulness and ability to improvise and do things in unexpected and creative ways

> awareness of and concern about everyday social and world issues.

Personality aspects of a gifted learning profile

The typical characteristics of a high-ability or gifted learning profile were described in Chapter 3. The personality aspects of these profiles draw on and elaborate on these (Gagné 2013; Subotnik et al. 2011). They include:

> an intrinsic motivation for excellence and a commitment and persistence to complete tasks

> determination, industry, well-developed self-regulation and the capacity to persevere to attain ends

> a strong need for mental activity and independence

> a preference for working alone

> self-efficacy, enthusiasm, boundless energy and curiosity for a subject

> emotional stability, emotional perceptiveness, tenacity and joy in achievement

> personal standards of intellectual activity and creativity, which students use to judge performance

> feelings of direction, harmony, beauty and style

> intuitive processes, intuition about problems, good ideas and elegant solutions.

For any student, you can collect data to identify these characteristics through structured interviews, in which you invite students to describe how each applies to them and to provide examples of each in their lives. You can also observe the extent to which students display these characteristics in their regular classroom learning.

Overexcitabilities

The Theory of Positive Disintegration (TPD) (Ackerman 2009) proposes that a higher responsiveness and sensitivity to sensory stimuli or 'overexcitabilities' (OEs) are associated with talent (Kane 2009). Five types of responsiveness or OE are assessed by this instrument:

1. Emotional: intense emotions, meaningful relationships, strong attachments
2. Imaginational: vivid imagery, use of metaphor, inventiveness, enjoyment of fantasy
3. Intellectual: enjoyment of problem-solving, avid reading, keen observation, love of theory
4. Psychomotor: love of movement, intense physical activity, impulsivity, restlessness
5. Sensual: delight in the beautiful, pleasure derived from the senses, overindulgence.

OEs are stronger among gifted individuals (Bouchet and Falk 2001) and can be measured using the Overexcitability Questionnaire II (Falk et al. 1999).

How to compile a high-ability or gifted learning profile

You can compile a high-ability learning or a gifted learning profile, by collating and comparing the assessment data from multiple sources. As discussed in Chapter 6, the first step in doing this is to convert the standard scores from normed tests and the raw scores and rating scores to percentile ranks. You can then see which tasks have scores in the high ability range (75th to 90th percentiles) and which are in the gifted learning range (90th and above percentiles). These ranges are recommended by Gagné (2020); Tests such as the Wechsler tests (Wechsler 2014) and the Stanford Binet (Roid 2003) recommend slightly different ranges and cut-off points based on the number of standard deviations from the mean. The gifted range of scores is sometimes further divided into the mildly gifted range (90th to 99th percentiles), the highly gifted range (99th to 99.9th percentiles), the exceptionally gifted range (99.9th to 99.99th), and the extremely or profoundly gifted range (99.9th to 99.99+th). Of course, not all assessments provide this level of precision in calculating scores.

Looking for patterns in the data

To compile a personal learning profile for a student, the first step involves looking for patterns in their data. The following set of questions can guide how you interpret their scores:

> ❯ In what areas does the student display talented outcomes ('talented' here refers to the quality of the outcomes, as noted in Chapter 6)? In which domains do they show an advanced breadth and depth of knowledge and the ability to think creativity? You can compare the student's scores of academic achievements on various tests and tasks in the domains.

> ❯ In what areas does the student show a gifted learning capacity? You can compare the student's scores on various types of tasks described in this chapter and in classroom learning activities to note those that are advanced. A student on the group reasoning scales may, for example, show verbal reasoning in the average range and imagery-spatial reasoning in the gifted range.

> ❯ What is the student's 'learning personality', in and beyond the classroom? This includes evidence of their task commitment and focus, and relevant emotional behaviours, such as high intrinsic motivation for excellence, perseverance and persistence, enthusiasm, cognitive curiosity and spontaneous enquiry. Teacher, parent/carer, peer and self-observational reports can inform this.

> ❯ What is the student's ability to monitor and independently self-regulate their learning? This includes how they plan,

implement and review their activity and how they select, organise and use the relevant information.

> What is the quality of the student's cultural and social interaction skills, including their range of social coping skills, the quality of their peer group interactions and their ability to learn collaboratively when necessary?

> What are characteristics of the student's identity as a gifted learner? This includes their self-efficacy, self-confidence, awareness of self and others, sense of integration as an individual and capacity to cope with emotional issues. Does the student show 'asynchronous development' in some areas; for example, high reasoning ability with immature social interaction skills?

A set of criteria for interpreting and combining the data from aptitude tests, performance tasks and achievement tasks is recommended by VanTassel-Baska and colleagues (VanTassel-Baska, Feng and de Brux 2007; VanTassel-Baska, Feng and Evans 2007). To be considered gifted, a student needs to meet one of 4 conditions. They score:

1. above the 94th percentile on an aptitude assessment scale
2. above the 90th percentile on an aptitude test and above the 94th percentile on an achievement test
3. above the 90th percentile on an aptitude test and above the 80th percentile on performance tasks
4. above the 94th percentile on an achievement test and above the 80th percentile on performance tasks.

This set offers schools a validated protocol for identifying high-ability and gifted students. Given the scope of this book to also include high achievers, schools could also use the 75th to 84th percentile range for one or more of aptitude tests, achievement tests and performance tasks to identify high achievers.

Interpreting scores in terms of individual student knowledge

As well as using students' numerical scores to identify if and how they are gifted, it is useful to interpret outcomes in terms of what they say about an individual student's knowledge and learning strengths. Numerical scores do not necessarily tell you all that a student might know about a topic or all they can do.

The second step in compiling a student's learning profile is to generate a description of each high-ability student's advanced knowledge and thinking ability. One student's profile, for example, may refer to a gifted verbal learning ability, with advanced vocabulary, a superior ability to analyse, evaluate, infer from and synthesise spoken and written texts, and to reason about and use symbolic systems, such as those in mathematics and science. A second student's profile may refer to a gifted non-verbal learning ability, with the superior capacity to think creatively and to infer laterally across a range of domains, to see unexpected implications in subjects such as history, science or English, and to solve a range of real-life problems innovatively. These descriptions can equip the teacher to differentiate the teaching more effectively and to use formative assessment procedures.

Online assessment of high ability

Online assessments are increasingly being used to assess students' strategic thinking skills. In a literature review, Periathiruvadi and Rinn (2012) describe the use of online assessments to identify high-ability learning profiles across a range of domains and contexts. They found that high-ability primary students used more sophisticated, high-level strategies in online gaming activities, used more effective self-regulation and focusing strategies, had higher memory capacity and were more self-motivated than their regular learning peers. High-ability secondary students used their time and on-task attention more effectively when completing computer-based assessments.

What your school can do now

Schools need valid and reliable procedures for identifying students who have high-ability learning profiles. These procedures need to identify multiple profiles. It is useful if staff know what the various tools measure, how they assess aspects of a high-ability profile and how to collate and interpret information, particularly in terms of how high-ability students learn.

Your school could run a workshop in which staff unpack how to identify an advanced learning capacity or aptitude in the verbal, imagery–spatial or practical performance domains and evaluate the extent to which existing procedures in the school already identify high ability and giftedness in these areas. To improve the identification procedures, your school could collect examples of assessment tasks and tools, such as observational checklists not currently used, and have staff identify the skills these tasks assess.

Some other recommended activities in which your school might engage are discussed here.

Design tasks to assess aspects of a high-ability learning profile

Staff can design tasks that they believe would assess the aspects of a high-ability and gifted learning profile, including the thinking characteristics linked with each profile. They can collaboratively evaluate the tasks created. It is recommended that this activity focus on the student attributes that need to be assessed for membership of each profile.

Evaluate current tasks and assessment procedures

Staff can work through the tasks and assessment procedures the school currently uses, identify the student attributes that are being assessed and compare these with the tasks they designed in the previous activity.

Staff can recommend how the set of procedures and tools used to identify the various high-ability and gifted profiles could be improved. This content can be used to create a set of criteria for 'ideal' identification practice. The perceptions of students and parents and carers could also inform this evaluation.

Collate high-ability and gifted profiles

Staff can be guided to interpret individual students' data and collate it into a high-ability and gifted profile. This could include interpreting data from teacher-developed tasks and open-ended assessments and converting them to percentile ranks.

If high ability and giftedness have been assessed in multiple areas (for example, in verbal, non-verbal and quantitative reasoning tasks, open-ended authentic tasks, problem-solving and creativity tasks and personality inventories), the areas in which the student does display high ability or giftedness can be identified.

To compare the outcomes from the various assessments, we need a way of interpreting the percentile ranks to see if each score is indicative of the gifted, high-ability, average-ability, low-ability or learning-difficulty range. We noted earlier that psychometricians differ in the specific percentile ranks that indicate the cut-offs for each range. This book uses Gagne's interpretation of the ranks and extends it as follows. Percentile ranks scores that are:

> at or above the 90th rank are in the gifted learning range

> between the 75th to 90th ranks are in the high-ability range

> between the 25th to 75th ranks are in the average-ability range

> between the 10th to 25th rank are in the low-ability range

> below the 10th rank are in the learning-difficulty range.

By comparing the relevant assessment outcomes, you can identify the areas in which the student displays:

> high-level or talented outcomes; for example, by comparing the student's academic achievement scores on various tests and on open-ended performance, authentic assessment and problem-solving tasks in various domains

> high-ability or gifted learning capacity; for example, by comparing the student's scores on various reasoning tests, the assessments of the quality of the thinking they display while working through the open-ended performance,

authentic assessment and problem-solving tasks, and the thinking they display during classroom learning

> aspects of high-ability or gifted learning personality; for example, by comparing ratings of their level of commitment and focus, intrinsic motivation, perseverance and persistence, enthusiasm, cognitive curiosity and spontaneous enquiry on open-ended tasks, ratings of the thinking they display during classroom learning and ratings from the parent/carer, peer and self-observational reports

> high or gifted ability to monitor and independently self-regulate by using ratings of their learning activity as they plan and work through open-ended tasks, the self-management they show in classroom learning activities and ratings from the parent/carer, peer and self-observational reports

> high or gifted ability to use a range of social interaction skills and to learn collaboratively

> an identity as a high-ability or gifted learner by using ratings of their self-efficacy, self-confidence, and capacity to cope with emotional issues.

One way of using this type of comparison is to look for evidence of 'asynchronous development' in students' knowledge and skills. Some high-ability and gifted students, for example, have high reasoning ability with immature social interaction skills.

Staff may benefit from workshops that unpack how to interpret the assessments performed by other professionals such as psychologists, to identify aspects of a student's learning profile and the implications of the assessment outcomes for implementing provision.

Identify underachieving high-ability and gifted students

Staff can be guided to interpret individual students' data where their learning profile is in the high-ability and gifted range and their outcomes or achievements are below it.

Teachers can analyse the gap or discrepancy between their learning profile scores and outcome scores in terms of possible causes. They can use percentile rank scores or other standard scores to do this. This comparison may, for example, indicate a twice-exceptional cause or social issues that lead students to mask or hide their high learning ability.

Interpret students' high-ability and gifted profiles formatively

Staff can be guided to interpret students' high-ability and gifted profiles formatively in terms of implications for future teaching. Assessment outcomes can be used to plan how to differentiate the curriculum, teaching and classroom culture, as discussed in Chapters 8 to 10. This type of professional learning activity allows schools to use assessment data to implement effective teaching and optimise learning.

Summary

As well as identifying high-level or talented outcomes, schools can also use assessments to identify a high-ability and gifted learning profile. Knowing this helps teachers understand how the students learn optimally and how to teach them. Some high-ability and gifted students do not display high-level outcomes, even though they have a high-ability and gifted learning profile.

Schools can identify high-ability and gifted learning profiles by:

> using standardised tests of reasoning skills, general ability, intelligence or aptitude. Both group and individually administered assessments are available. These tests will indicate high-ability and gifted learning in the verbal and the imagery–spatial or non-verbal areas

> using open-ended authentic assessments tasks to identify imagery–spatial, practical and twice-exceptional profiles. Performance on these tasks can be assessed using appropriate rubrics

> using assessments of the ability and motivation to think creatively; this is referred to as 'creative potential'

› monitoring a student's overall approach to learning in the classroom and by using teacher, peer and student ratings

› assessing students' personality characteristics.

The assessment context can be modified to identify the profiles of twice-exceptional students.

Teachers can compile a high-ability and gifted learning profile by collating and comparing assessment data from multiple sources.

References

ACER (Australian Council for Educational Research) (2023a) *General Ability Test (AGAT)*, Australian Council for Educational Research, Melbourne, Victoria, accessed 30 October 2023. https://www.acer.org/au/agat/assessment

ACER (Australian Council for Educational Research) (2023b) *Higher Ability Selection Test – Secondary*, Australian Council for Educational Research, Melbourne, Victoria, accessed 30 October 2023. https://www.acer.org/hast-secondary

ACER (Australian Council for Educational Research) (2005) *Middle Years Ability Test (MYAT)*, Australian Council for Educational Research, Melbourne, Victoria, accessed 30 October 2023. https://www.acer.org/ae/tsa/middle-years-ability-test-myat

Ackerman CM (2009) 'The essential elements of Dabrowski's theory of positive disintegration and how they are connected', *Roeper Review*, 31(2):81–95, doi:10.1080/02783190902737657.

Barbot B, Besançon M and Lubart T (2011) 'Assessing creativity in the classroom', *Open Education Journal*, 4:58–66.

Bakx A, Samsen-Bronsveld E, van Elderen L and van Horssen-Sollie J (2021) 'Self-descriptions of high-performing and regular-performing primary school students: an open, exploratory study', *Roeper Review*, 43(4):256–271, doi:10.1080/02783193.2021.1967543.

Bouchet NM and Falk RF (2001) 'The relationship among giftedness, gender, and overexcitability', *Gifted Child Quarterly*, 45:260–267, doi:10.1177/001698620104500404.

Cropley AJ (2000) 'Defining and measuring creativity: are creativity tests worth using?', *Roeper Review*, 23(2):72–79, doi:10.1080/02783190009554069.

Falk RF, Lind S, Miller NB, Piechowski MM and Silverman LK (1999) *The Overexcitabilities Questionnaire-Two (OEQII)*, Institute for the Study of Advanced Development, Denver, CO.

Feldhusen JF, Hoover SM and Sayler MF (1990) *Identifying and educating gifted students at the secondary level*, Unionville, Trillium Press, New York.

Gagné F (2013) 'The DMGT: changes within, beneath, and beyond', *Talent Development and Excellence*, 5(1):5–19.

Gagné F (2020) *Differentiating giftedness from talent: the DMGT perspective on talent development*, Routledge, New York, doi:10.4324/9781003088790.

Gilliam JE, Carpenter BO and Christensen JR (1996) *Gifted and talented evaluation scales: a norm-referenced procedure for identifying gifted and talented students*, PRO-ED, Austin, TX.

Kane M (2009) 'Contemporary voices on Dabrowski's theory of positive disintegration', *Roeper Review*, 31:72–76.

Lakin JM (28 January 2019) 'The essentials: using ability tests in gifted and talented identification programs', *Riverside Insights Blog*, Riverside Insights, Rolling Meadows, Illinois, accessed 30 October 2023. https://blog.riversideinsights.com/ability-tests-gifted-talented-identification-programs

Lidz CS and Macrine SL (2001) 'An alternative approach to the identification of gifted culturally and linguistically diverse learners: the contribution of dynamic assessment, *School Psychology International*, 22(1):74–96.

Lubart TI, Besançon M and Barbot B (2011) *Evaluation of creative potential: test and manual*, Editions Hogrefe France, Paris.

McCallum MS and Bracken B (2018) *Universal Talented and Gifted Screener*, Routledge, Oxfordshire.

McCarney SB and Arthaud TJ (2009) *Gifted evaluation scale third edition (GES-3)*, Hawthorne Educational Services, Columbia, MO.

Mednick SA (1962) 'The associative basis of the creative process', *Psychological Review*, 69:220–232.

Periathiruvadi S and Rinn AN (2012) 'Technology in gifted education', *Journal of Research on Technology in Education,* 45(2):153–169, doi:10.1080/15391523.2012.10782601.

Plucker JA (1999) 'Is the proof in the pudding? Reanalysis of Torrance's (1958 to present) longitudinal data', *Creativity Research Journal*, 12:103–114.

Raven JC, Court JH and Raven J (1992) *Manual for Raven's Progressive Matrices and Mill Hill Vocabulary scales*, Oxford Psychologists Press, Oxford.

Renzulli JS, Smith LH, White AJ, Callahan CM, Hartman RK and Westberg KL (2002) *Scales for rating the behavior characteristics of superior students: revised edition*, Creative Learning Press, Mansfield Center, CT.

Rimm S, Gilman B and Silverman L (2008) 'Alternative assessments with gifted and talented students', *Nontraditional Applications of Traditional Testing*, 175–202.

Roid GH and Pomplun (2012) *The Stanford-Binet Intelligence Scales* (Vol. 654), The Guilford Press, New York.

Ryser GR and McConnell K (2004) *Scales for identifying gifted students: ages 5 through 18*, Prufrock Press, Waco, TX.

Subotnik RF, Olszewski-Kubilius P and Worrell FC (2011) 'Rethinking giftedness and gifted education. A proposed direction forward based on psychological science, *Psychological Science in the Public Interest*, 12(1):3–54.

Torrance EP (1972) 'Career patterns and peak creative achievements of creative high school students 12 years later', *Gifted Child Quarterly*, 16:75–88.

Torrance EP (1999) *Torrance Test of Creative Thinking: norms and technical manual*, Scholastic Testing Services, Beaconville, IL.

Urban KK and Jellen HG (1996) *Test for Creative Thinking – drawing production (tct-dp)*, Swets and Zeitlinger, Lisse, Netherlands.

VanTassel-Baska J, Feng AX and de Brux E (2007) 'A study of identification and achievement profiles of performance task-identified gifted students over 6 years', *Journal for the Education of the Gifted*, 31(1):7–34.

VanTassel-Baska J, Feng AX and Evans BL (2007) 'Patterns of identification and performance among gifted students identified through performance tasks: a three-year analysis', *Gifted Child Quarterly*, 51(3):218–231.

Wallach MA and Kogan N (1965) *Modes of thinking in young children*, Rinehart and Winston, Holt, New York.

Wechsler D (2014) *Wechsler Intelligence Scale for Children (5th ed.)*, PsychCorp, Bloomington, MN.

Worrell FC and Erwin JO (2011) 'Best practices in identifying students for gifted and talented education programs', *Journal of Applied School Psychology*, 27(4):319–340.

CHAPTER 8

How to differentiate the regular curriculum

Introduction

High-ability students are more likely to achieve high-level outcomes when the teaching lets them know that these are expected – that is, when the teaching targets these outcomes. This requires teachers to know what the high-level outcomes might 'look like', as discussed in Chapter 2. It also requires regular classroom provision to be modified. This differentiation includes modifying what is taught, how it is taught, the context for teaching and how the student shows what they have learnt (the product) (Tomlinson and Moon 2013).

Why do school leaders and middle leaders need to know about differentiation? Chandra Handa (2019) notes that principals' understanding of differentiated learning for high-ability and gifted students informs how effectively schoolwide differentiation is implemented. A deep understanding of differentiation equips principals to lead and guide teachers' own differentiation practices and to actively lead enhanced provision.

This chapter examines how to differentiate what the student will learn; that is, the content or curriculum. Chapters 9 and 10 respectively go on to examine how to differentiate teaching to match how the student will learn, and the context and culture in which the learning happens.

The main ideas in this chapter are shown in in Figure 8.1.

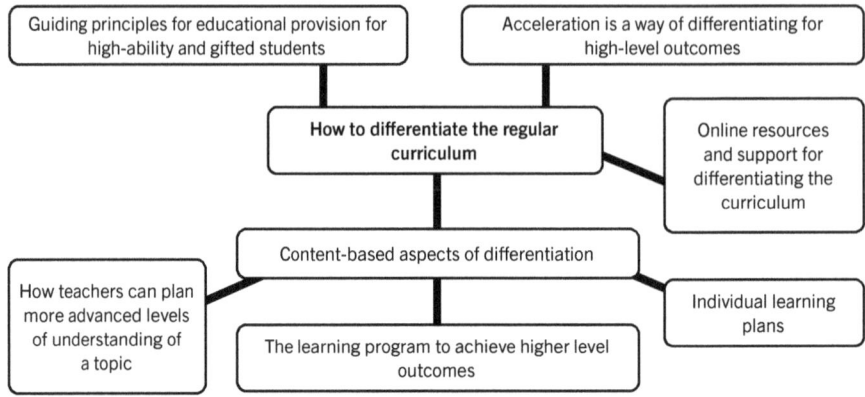

Figure 8.1. Differentiating the regular curriculum for high-ability and gifted students

Principles for educational provision for high-ability and gifted students

In a synthesis of the research on educational provision for high-ability and gifted students, Rogers (2007:382) provides leaders with a set of 5 principles or 'lessons' to guide their improvement agenda. Broadly, these recommend that the following opportunities be provided to high-ability and gifted students:

1. daily challenges in areas of talent
2. regular chances to be unique and learn independently in areas of interest and talent
3. subject-based and year-level acceleration
4. opportunities to socialise and learn with like-ability peers
5. teaching differentiated in pace, review and practice and content presentation.

These principles provide a foundation for curriculum provision, inform the recommendations for curriculum, teaching and culture and climate in this and the following 2 chapters and are briefly reviewed here.

1. Provide daily challenges in areas of talent

This can be done through complex provocations or problems, often in collaborative learning activities with like-ability peers and/or with mentors. The challenges can lead to advanced knowledge and understanding.

The teaching content needs to be aligned with the provocations and needs to be appropriately sophisticated or advanced. This provision can impact the workload of teachers and leadership may need to reflect on how high-ability and gifted students can be offered an appropriately challenging curriculum beyond the regular classroom context.

2. Provide regular chances to be unique and learn independently in areas of interest and talent

High-ability and gifted students often prefer the freedom to pursue their intuitive theories about what they are learning and to be self-teachers. To do this, they need a range of independent learning capacities, such as task commitment and motivation to learn, metacognitive skills, self-efficacy and self-reliance, the ability to frame up goals for learning, and appropriate critical and creative thinking skills. The preference for independence needs to be balanced with the opportunity to learn interactively and to be taught by others. High-ability students value this balance. This is unpacked in more depth in Chapter 12.

The need for both directed teaching and independent learning opportunity is important for twice-exceptional students. Chapter 5 noted that these students may have difficulty using the required literacy and/or study skills or in engaging emotionally with the teaching information.

Leaders may need to reflect on how they provide the support needed for effective independent learning and self-teaching in the classroom. One format for this is online instruction. Curriculum development models that offer independent study provisions include Betts et al.'s (2016) Autonomous Learner Model and Renzulli's and Renzulli's (2010) Enrichment Triad/Schoolwide Enrichment Model, which are discussed further on (see p. 142).

3. Provide opportunities for subject-based and year-level acceleration

This principle can encompass opportunities such as early entry to kindergarten or primary school, subject acceleration, advanced placement and dual enrolment in university courses. These are unpacked later in this chapter.

4. Provide opportunities to socialise and to learn with like-ability peers

High-ability and gifted students learn better and have more positive self-efficacy when they are in like-ability groups. This can include full-time ability grouping, grouping for specific domains and within-class grouping with differentiated teaching. The within-class grouping is more effective than no grouping or mixed-ability classrooms, as long as the curriculum and learning tasks are differentiated. These opportunities are elaborated further on.

Some schools offer the opportunity for learning with 'like-minded' students by implementing or engaging in withdrawal programs in which the students learn in contexts away from their regular classrooms. Rogers (2007) notes that students in the withdrawal contexts achieve at a higher level than matched students who are not withdrawn. Rogers (2007) attributes this difference to several causes: the teaching information in the withdrawal group usually includes more sophisticated content, the teachers in the withdrawal context are usually better prepared and equipped to teach these students than regular teachers and the students are more aware that their high-ability learning programs are being targeted. In other words, the gains in the withdrawal context may not be due only to the context per se, but to other factors.

5. Provide teaching that is differentiated in pace, review and practice, and content presentation

Each of the aspects of differentiation Rogers (2007) mentions in this 'lesson' is worthy of separate definition.

Pace

High-ability and gifted students should ideally be taught at the rate at which they learn. One way this can be supported is via online teaching.

Teachers can also include procedures for monitoring students' learning outcomes so they can 'see' changes in students' knowledge more readily and modify their teaching accordingly. They can invite student feedback and use this to shape and differentiate the subsequent teaching and provide the opportunity for these students to learn in bigger steps. They can also provide increased opportunities for these students to manage and direct parts of their learning activity and to be self-teachers.

Less practice and review

High-ability and gifted students need less practice to master and recall what they have learnt. Learning through more advanced inquiry and problem-solving can replace practice and review activities for them.

Content presentation: teach the 'big idea' before detail

'Regular' students learn a concept by progressing from the parts to the whole. High-ability and gifted students often learn a new concept by first forming an initial overall impression or intuitive theory about it and then considering the parts. Sternberg's (1986) descriptions of gifted mathematicians and scientists as 'decontextualists' exemplify this. They form a general idea from a specific problem. He contrasted this with 'constructivists' who think by assembling parts into a whole.

School leadership can reflect on how they can lead teachers to differentiate their provision to match the 'whole-to-part' thinking used by these students.

Acceleration is a way of differentiating for high-level outcomes

Some students, via their learning profiles and the high-level knowledge they have formed through earlier intuitive theory of action activity, can learn content that is usually taught at a higher year level. Curriculum differentiation gives them this opportunity. They are exposed to more complex and sophisticated content and form intuitive theories of action that in turn lead to the high-level outcomes.

One approach to giving these students this opportunity is through academic or content acceleration. Students progress through educational programs either at rates faster than or at ages younger than their peers (Steenbergen-Hu and Moon 2011). This can include being placed in a class with older students or curriculum modifications that lead to differentiated learning experiences within regular classrooms.

A nation deceived: how schools hold back America's brightest students (Colangelo et al. 2004) describes 18 types of acceleration. These include:

> - locating the student in a higher year where more advanced knowledge is being taught for all or part of their learning (whole-year and subject-specific acceleration)
> - teaching at the student's rate of learning, controlled by the teacher or student (self-paced)
> - modifying or 'compacting' the curriculum; for example, reducing the extent of introductory activity and/or practice, or teaching in larger increments
> - a withdrawal program that teaches other topics and may involve working with mentors, extracurricular programs and correspondence courses
> - credentialing the gifted student's advanced knowledge in various ways; for example, the student studies subjects at an earlier age
> - the student entering school or university at an age earlier than their same-age peers
> - the student learning more complex and advanced knowledge than their peers in same-age classrooms.

These acceleration procedures are sometimes called 'appropriate developmental placements' (Lubinski and Benbow 2000:138). Whatever the acceleration protocol, differentiated teaching can scaffold students to pursue more advanced curriculum goals for topics or domains.

The follow-up report *A nation empowered: evidence trumps the excuses holding back America's brightest students* (Assouline et al. 2015) is a useful sequel to *A nation deceived*. It describes the various types of academic acceleration and their social and emotional impacts on the lives of gifted students, the long-term effects and their implementation with twice-exceptional students. This follow-up report provides useful guidelines for developing an acceleration policy. It recommends that the policy is equitable, with access to acceleration available to all students who display high-ability or gifted learning profiles, and describes how the acceleration will be implemented and how it will be administered to ensure fair and systematic application. Rogers (2015) reports effect sizes of the various types of acceleration described in the report, for primary and secondary students.

Some educators have raised concerns about options that physically separate the high-ability and gifted students from same-age peers. However, some research suggests that generally this is not harmful and has small to moderate social–emotional benefits (Rogers 2015; Steenbergen-Hu and Moon 2011).

Acceleration generally benefits both academic outcomes and social–emotional development for gifted students (Steenbergen-Hu and Moon 2011). Enrichment programs, withdrawal programs and placement in special classes, for example, positively influence gifted students' academic achievement and socioemotional development (Kim 2016; Vaughn et al. 1991).

Obviously, the year levels of the students and types of programs affect the outcomes. The research reporting the positive outcomes of acceleration also often doesn't take account of teachers' professional knowledge about how to provide for high-ability and gifted students. Simply teaching higher level content, and assuming that these students learn in much the same way as their older peers, may not be sufficient for some students and may reduce the likelihood of talented outcomes being realised. Rogers' (2007) principles for educational provision for these students indicate that regular teaching is often insufficient for achieving these outcomes.

Chapter 3 noted that high-ability and gifted students can learn higher level content and interpret it differently. It is these different interpretations that lead to talented outcomes. Teachers who understand how these students learn are more likely to provide the opportunity and classroom climate for the accelerated student to explicate and investigate their intuitive theories of action and so achieve optimal outcomes.

The acceleration program for any high-ability and gifted student needs to be aligned with their learning profile. Whole-year acceleration, for example, is not appropriate for all high-ability and gifted students. Students with uneven academic profiles benefit from acceleration in the area of their strength. Schools can be assisted to make decisions here using scales such as the Iowa Acceleration Scale (IAS) (Assouline et al. 2009). These scales use data relating to developmental factors, social skills, student attitudes and support from parents and carers and school.

School leaders can also use the Guidelines for Accelerated Progression (Board of Studies NSW 2000) to decide high-ability and gifted students' suitability for accelerated progression. These guidelines are derived from Feldhusen et al. (1986) and recommend the following questions:

> - Does comprehensive psychological assessment of intellectual functioning, academic skill levels and social-emotional adjustment support acceleration?
> - Does the student show above-average academic skill in the class in which they seek to be located?
> - Does the student show evidence of serious social and emotional adjustment problems?
> - Does the student have good physical health?
> - Is the student keen to move to the higher year versus feeling unduly pressured by parents or carers to do so?
> - Does the receiving teacher have positive attitudes towards the year advancement and are they willing to help the student adjust to the new situation?
> - Do the student's parents or carers and the psychologist judge the student to be socially and emotionally mature?
> - Is the year advancement occurring at a natural transition point, such as the beginning of the school year? Is the student's transition likely to be smooth?

> Will the accelerated progression operate for a trial basis of at least 2 months? Is the student accepting of the trial period and its consequences?

> How are the expectations from year advancement managed and contained? (Board of Studies NSW 2000)

Some students may also need to be prepared or 'readied' for acceleration. Some students may have concerns about possible issues in the accelerated context and others may need to alternate between their existing situation and the accelerated contexts.

Content-based aspects of differentiation

Either in addition to or as an alternative to exposing high-ability and gifted students to existing higher level content, teachers may sometimes need to generate more complex content to set more advanced goals and expectations for these students. This allows the students to learn more complex and advanced knowledge in classrooms with their same-age peers. This is 'within class' differentiation (Rogers 2007).

This differentiation is more successful when the teacher understands high-ability and gifted learning profiles. The teacher modifies or 'compacts' the curriculum for particular domains; for example, taking account of what the students already know about a topic, and gives these students the opportunity to learn faster or in larger increments than their peers.

Teachers can create versions of higher level curriculum knowledge by selecting content that is at a higher year level in the regular curriculum (that is, differentiating 'upwards'). This includes taking account of what the students already know about a topic, reducing the practice they need, teaching in larger increments of knowledge or allowing them to learn at their own rate.

Planning for more advanced levels of understanding

To plan the higher levels of knowledge and skill high-ability and gifted students will learn, the teacher can either select and use existing content that is taught at a higher year or create more sophisticated and advanced versions of content they are teaching to regular students. Both are versions of whole-year or subject-specific acceleration and include 'compacting the curriculum'.

To plan and create more advanced versions of the knowledge and differentiate the curriculum, teachers can:

1. specify explicitly what the regular students will learn
2. identify and select the key concepts and ideas
3. frame up a higher level of understanding of the concepts and ideas by thinking about them divergently
4. imagine how each concept might change; and infer more complex, advanced relationships or outcomes
5. analyse and evaluate the advanced ideas in terms of their appropriateness for the students
6. synthesise the possible relationships into a theory – this is the more advanced understanding the high-ability and gifted students can learn; it may match topics already in the curriculum
7. describe the target understanding as a curriculum goal.

Some examples of 'differentiating up' topics are presented in the following year 7 and year 6 scenarios.

Scenarios

Year 7 class

A year 7 class is learning about the structure of leaves, the functions that occur and the ingredients of the photosynthesis reaction. The higher levels of understanding for high-ability and gifted students could include questions and topics such as:

› How might the features of leaves (their shape, size, thickness) affect photosynthesis? Which plants photosynthesise more efficiently?

> How might the efficiency and rate of photosynthesis be affected by more or less light, hotter or colder conditions or climate change? What environmental conditions best favour photosynthesis?

> How does photosynthesis occur in aquatic plants?

> How does the photosynthesis reaction occur in plant cells and how have plant cells adapted to accommodate it?

Year 6 class

A year 6 class is learning how the author of a particular narrative uses language and text structure to achieve humour. The higher levels of understanding a teacher could plan for high-ability and gifted students include:

> how different language and text structures communicate different types of humour

> how different types of humour achieve different purposes and goals

> how and why factors such as the age of characters in a text, their power relationship with others, technology or their culture affect the type of humour in a text and when humour has a positive or negative effect

> rules for writing humorous texts in multiple genres

> ethical and moral aspects of using humour; when does it 'overstep the mark'?

Teachers can use a similar procedure to those discussed in the classroom scenarios to generate higher levels of understanding for any topic they are teaching.

Planning teaching and learning for higher level outcomes

Teachers also need to plan the teaching and learning program that leads students to the higher level outcomes. This includes tasks that lead students to learn more complex and sophisticated ideas about the topic. The teaching program may comprise 2 components:

1. A differentiated **teaching** component. The teacher differentiates their regular classroom teaching by including prompts and cues that guide students to think about the teaching at the higher level. This scaffolds students with high-ability and gifted profiles to begin to form more advanced interpretations.

2. A differentiated **curriculum** component in which these students learn the higher-level knowledge outcomes, while their peers pursue the regular curriculum. This combines teacher-directed activity and autonomous student-directed learning and can be structured as a project that extends the regular content.

These are versions of general curriculum modification or differentiation. The learning program can include either or both components, depending on students' existing knowledge. Students judged to have high-level existing knowledge of the topic may begin with the curriculum component. Other students may not work well in self-directed contexts and can instead be involved largely through the differentiated teaching component. The differentiated teaching component is elaborated in Chapter 9.

Teaching differentiated curriculum content

This curriculum component can be implemented as a student-managed project, guiding them to investigate their intuitive theory about the topic in a systematic, manageable way that leads to knowledge extension.

Teachers may need guidance in doing this. The following sequence of 12 questions can be used to plan differentiated curriculum outcomes in any domain for high-ability and gifted students and can inform leaders' discussion with teachers about this. The steps also comprise an Individual Learning Program or ILP for high-ability and gifted students.

1. How will you organise the knowledge pathway?

When teachers have decided the knowledge or skills to be learnt, they can break it into a sequence of steps. This is the 'knowledge pathway'. The teacher and student together can use techniques such as brainstorming or concept mapping to plan the sequence. They can negotiate a written 'contract' that specifies what will be achieved at each step. They can use this to monitor progress and to modify it when appropriate.

2. How will you identify students who have the existing knowledge needed?

The teacher plans the pre-teaching assessment procedures they will use. To do this they can:

> identify explicitly the learning outcomes to be achieved

> identify the assumed or prerequisite knowledge needed and assess this.

3. How will you challenge students to engage in the project?

Teachers can create complex provocations, such as 'scenario' problems that probe the topic, and present these to the students. These problems are open-ended and often in 'real-world' settings. The students need to clarify them. Examples of scenario problems are included here.

Scenario problems

For the English goal of humour

How do different genres of writing, such as a narrative, a poem, a jingle, or an advertisement, use language and text structure to achieve different types of humour? What is the best genre for communicating sarcasm, dry humour and witty humour?

For the Science goal of photosynthesis

How might climate change in the next 20 years affect the cell structure in plants and the chemistry of photosynthesis?

4. What are the necessary information sources and learning activities?

Students learn by using a range of information sources and activities that match the knowledge pathway. These include online and real-world sources that can incorporate combinations of written and spoken text, visual and imagery forms, action and physical forms, such as demonstrations.

Some high-ability and gifted students, including many who are twice exceptional, may need guidance or individual assistance in using these information sources and associated skills; for example, how to:

> use information, research and reference skills; this includes locating and selecting possible sources, planning and using collection and organising skills

> observe or listen strategically (such as when learning from a video) or how to interview a speaker, such as a mentor; this includes being able to use study skills, such as taking notes and outlining, summarising and prioritising

> read with comprehension; again using study skills

> use specialised perceptual-motor skills; this includes skills using tools and equipment in science and technology and the creative arts, keyboards and computer and information technology.

5. How will you guide students to create and evaluate their intuitive theories?

The teaching can scaffold students to think in various ways about the content to build their understanding. It can direct them to:

> identify or frame up possible problems that interpret and unpack provocative questions or challenging issues and plan how they might investigate and solve them. The teacher can guide students to plan a sequence of smaller, intermediate questions that lead to the bigger problem. These questions indicate the steps in the knowledge pathway described in step 1 of this list of questions (see p. 136)

> examine the topic and ideas from multiple perspectives; for example, using De Bono's Six Hats; Plus, Minus, Interesting (PMI) or KWHL procedures (De Bono 1982; Kivunja 2015; Sukarno 2019)

> experiment with their thinking; unpack ideas that are perplexing and barriers to learning at any time; explore organising, linking and prioritising ideas in multiple ways; use brainstorming and concept mapping

> examine apparently ambiguous, inconsistent, contradictory or controversial aspects from multiple perspectives; analyse, compare, contrast and evaluate ideas

> infer patterns and relationships, think divergently and flexibly and explore possibilities and consequences by asking 'what if …', 'if … then …' and 'how might/could' questions

> make links across subjects and domains, synthesise their understanding and apply it in different contexts.

Students can use the various types of thinking strategies selectively on an 'as needed' basis according to the task demands at the time.

6. In what context(s) will the students learn?

The students can learn in several contexts in and beyond the classroom. This includes some of the acceleration contexts mentioned earlier. Select those that are most appropriate for the activity at any time.

7. How will you group high-ability and gifted students to learn throughout this component?

Flexible groupings are recommended in regular classroom contexts.

8. How will you support students to learn independently?

Teachers can plan how they will give students the opportunity to use their metacognition, self-agency and intrinsic motivation and to show task commitment to guide their activity. Ways in which teachers can encourage independence include giving students the opportunity to contribute to planning the knowledge pathway, unpacking and recording what they already know about the topic, deciding the types of information sources they will use, and monitoring their own progress. Students can also be encouraged to 'tell the story' of their high-ability and gifted understanding of the issue.

9. How will you guide students to monitor regularly what they have learnt?

As they progress along the pathway, students can consolidate what they have learnt and how it contributes to the final or terminal goal. Teachers decide how they will monitor student progress and provide regular feedback to the student and other stakeholders, including parents or carers and other teachers.

10. How will students display their understanding?

Students can show their understanding in multiple formats:

> a literary format: a written investigation or research report, an essay, opinion, narrative, instruction manual or article

> a spoken format: a speech, debate, story, instructions, discussion, poem or values statement

> a production format: a construction, model, invention, sculpture, simulation, puzzle or exhibit

> a demonstration: a practical performance, drama, puppet show or game

> a pictorial or image-based format: a visual or graphic representation, painting, cartoon, diagram, video, map, illustration or photograph

> information technology format: an e-text, innovative computer game, an app, a multimedia presentation or a computer program.

Some students, including those who are twice exceptional, may need to improve their skill to prepare or compose oral or written outcomes. Some outcomes will be 'multimodal'; they will use multiple contexts to communicate their understanding.

11. How will you assess students' responses to the differentiated curriculum unit?

Throughout this book, high ability and gifted learning has been described in terms of the intuitive theories some students form about the teaching information. These theories contain more ideas than what were in the teaching. You assess students' responses by noting the number of additional ideas and how these are linked, both with the ideas in the teaching and other additional ideas. You can write a rubric that examines whether the student's outcome shows evidence of:

- inferred additional separate ideas
- inferred additional ideas linked into possible causal or consequential relationships
- inferred rules or general propositions about the topic
- creative and evaluative perspectives on the topic
- possible moral or ethical issues about the topic
- inferred 'big ideas' for the topic.

To assist you to do this, you can identify, for the topic, possible outcomes that would be indicative of thinking at each level.

12. How will students use their understanding to enhance peer group knowledge?

High-ability and gifted students' regular peers are often learning the same general topic. The opportunity to share new knowledge with peers helps high-ability and gifted students improve their skill in communicating their advanced understanding. Their presentations model high-ability and gifted thinking about the topic and this can also extend the regular students' knowledge. You can scaffold these students to plan how they will do this. You can guide them to:

- collate what they have learnt
- organise it in a form that makes it easy to share with peers; plan how to share it
- select formats that allow them to do this; some options are described in step 10.

Examples of the differentiated curriculum component

One example of this type of project is the Type III Enrichment aspect of the Enrichment Triad Model (part of the School Enrichment Model) developed by Renzulli and Renzulli (2010) for talent development with gifted students. Type III Enrichment provides the opportunity to form a more advanced and sophisticated understanding of topics in the regular curriculum though investigation, and creative and critical thinking.

The School Enrichment Model aims to develop a range of personal characteristics in high-ability and gifted learners, including:

> optimism (hope, positive feelings from hard work)

> sensitivity to human concerns (insight, empathy)

> courage (psychological/intellectual independence, moral conviction)

> physical/mental energy (charisma, curiosity)

> vision/sense of destiny (sense of power to change things, sense of direction, pursuit of passion)

> romance with a topic or discipline (absorption, goals).

McCann (2003) added a modification to the Enrichment Triad. It encourages students to evaluate and reflect on the Type III Enrichment investigation after it has been completed, to:

> make links with other areas of knowledge for further study

> redefine problems and ask new questions

> be metacognitive about their thinking and learning – what worked, what was difficult or easy to learn and what could be improved

> reflect on the positive behaviours (habits of mind) that helped them to be successful.

This evaluation leads to further learning and possibly further enquiry and learning activity.

A second example of this curriculum differentiation is the 'In-depth study' in the *Autonomous learner model: optimizing ability* developed by Betts et al. (2016) for gifted and talented students. It can be used in specific curriculum areas in the regular classroom, in small group settings, in a withdrawal or resource context or in individual study. It aims to guide students to be autonomous learners who can manage and direct the learning process, with teachers operating as facilitators of learning. It comprises 5 dimensions:

1. Orientation: students develop an understanding of the concepts of high-level and talented outcomes. They learn more about themselves and their abilities.

2. Individual development: students develop the cognitive, emotional, social and physical skills, as well as concepts and attitudes necessary for lifelong learning.

3. Enrichment: students implement an investigative project and engage in cultural events in the community.

4. Seminars: students share the outcomes of their research with others.

5. In-depth study: students engage in an in-depth study in which they specify:

    - what and how they will learn
    - the resources they need
    - how they will evaluate the learning process
    - how they will share it.

A learning contract can be used to support this dimension.

Online learning and the differentiated curriculum

Online learning offers the opportunity for providing a differentiated curriculum. Online educational provision has grown exponentially over the last 2 decades (Potts and Potts 2017). Programs such as Massive Open Online Courses (MOOCs) (Deng et al. 2019) and the Khan

Academy (Arnavut et al. 2019) can contribute to high-ability and gifted provision. Online and traditional provision have also been combined into blended or hybrid learning models. These models allow students to self-pace with teacher direction and provide opportunities for group projects and assignments, as well as virtual class meetings.

The online and blended formats can often facilitate individualised, differentiated learning experiences for high-ability and gifted students more successfully than face-to-face in a regular classroom (Swan et al. 2015; Thomson 2011). Many of these students prefer to learn online because this format can provide a more complex curriculum with more learning challenges than the classroom, the opportunity to self-direct and manage their learning activity and greater self-pacing and flexibility (Olszewski-Kubilius and Lee 2004).

One type of blended learning is the 'flipped classroom' format, in which students learn content by watching video lessons prior to studying the content in the classroom. In one study, academic high-achieving secondary students preferred it over traditional face-to-face instruction (Gelgoot et al. 2020). The students in the flipped lesson context did not differ in achievement from the traditional class but showed higher engagement with the topic and rated organisation, clarity and enjoyment higher.

It is possible that the emerging artificial intelligence (AI) platforms can play a valuable role here. Their capacity to summarise and to identify possible unanswered issues or questions may assist in generating higher levels of understanding for a topic and challenging questions for high-ability students to explore. When presented with suitable prompts, these platforms may also recommend assessment criteria that can indicate high-level critical and creative thinking.

Sanderson and Greenberger (2011) recommend the following criteria schools can use to evaluate online teaching programs in terms of their suitability for high-ability and gifted learners:

> ❯ Has the program been designed specifically for high-ability and gifted students; for example, does it permit self-pacing, provide challenge and balance set learning pathways with opportunities for student-directed learning?

> Does it introduce students appropriately to the learning context?

> Do its objectives match the student's learning objectives and does it adequately either replace or enrich regular classroom provision?

> Do its activities and assignments have complexity and rigour and foster creative thinking and problem-solving skills?

> How is the curriculum delivered; for example, what is the balance between synchronous and asynchronous activities, and the use of multimedia, such as videos and animation, versus text-based reading and writing?

> Are the self-direction and management skills and organisational and time-management skills required by the program clearly specified and appropriate for the student?

> Are the entry knowledge and skills the program assumes and the procedures it uses to assess them appropriate for the student?

> How is feedback provided; for example, what is its frequency, immediacy and quality, both summative and formative?

> How easily can a student's teacher(s) interact with or modify the provision to differentiate learning; for example, can they add content, modify the presentation of the information or include tests and quizzes?

> Does the program assist these students to learn collaboratively; for example, through synchronous virtual meetings, group project work and problem-solving, discussion boards and chat rooms?

> How are student outcomes assessed; for example, do they include performance-based, product-based and standardised assessments? Are these differentiated to match individual students' learning profiles?

> What hardware and software are required for curriculum delivery and how are student–teacher interactions facilitated?

Potts and Potts (2017) provide a set of criteria for deciding whether a high-ability or gifted student is suited for online learning. These ask, does the student have:

> the necessary technical, computer and online skills

> persistence, flexibility, adaptability and an interest in online learning

> the necessary reading comprehension and other literacy research skills

> the ability to learn independently, direct their learning activity, maintain focus and resist distractions, and use a schedule to manage commitments

> the ability to engage maturely with others in an online environment?

What your school can do now

An important aspect of educational provision for high-ability and gifted students is access to curriculum that takes account of all that they know and that provides the opportunity for them to enhance this. These students are more likely to achieve high-level and talented outcomes when the curriculum to which they are exposed targets more advanced and sophisticated knowledge and skills.

This section examines how you can evaluate your school's current practices in curriculum differentiation for these students and how this might be improved.

Evaluate your school's current practices in curriculum differentiation

Teachers can analyse and evaluate Rogers' (2007) 5 principles in terms of what each would look like in regular teaching in your school. They can infer how these could be mapped into classroom practice and implemented.

They can use the content in this chapter, including Rogers' principles, to develop a checklist for evaluating their current practice in curriculum differentiation. They can use this checklist to monitor and evaluate the use of curriculum differentiation procedures in their current practice.

Decide on acceleration procedures

The leadership, possibly in dialogue with teachers, can decide which of the various types of acceleration it will adopt as an approach to achieving curriculum differentiation and for whom. Teachers can reflect on how they would make placement and acceleration decisions and how they would evaluate the effectiveness of differentiated curriculum options for individual students.

Decide how to differentiate the curriculum

Teachers can identify how they can use ready-made higher level content for high-ability and gifted students and how they can generate higher level content for topics they teach.

Practise developing advanced curriculum topics and content

Teachers can practice applying the 12 points described earlier in the 'Teaching differentiated curriculum' section to content they will teach. It is recommended that teachers have the opportunity to learn how to:

> 'upwardly' differentiate topics they will teach and identify more complex knowledge and skill goals for the higher ability students

> plan their learning pathways to the differentiated curriculum goals

> design 'open-ended' learning tasks that draw on the thinking that typifies high-ability and gifted learning (for example, inferential, divergent, analytic and synthetic thinking)

> plan how to assess the higher levels of understanding

> plan activities in which students share their new knowledge with peers and the broader community, having learnt the skills needed to collate and communicate the outcomes of their learning.

Extend availability of high-ability and gifted programs

Your school can also review the range of high-ability and gifted learning profiles in the school and decide whether the opportunity for involvement in high-ability and gifted programs needs to be broadened and extended.

To do this, teachers can evaluate the curriculum differentiation modifications they have decided to make and examine whether these adequately accommodate all types of high-ability and gifted learning profiles in the school. The school might decide to pursue the goal that all students with high-ability or gifted learning profiles can access programs that target a differentiated curriculum. Twice-exceptional students may need curriculum modifications that take account of the second exceptionality.

Summary

Rogers (2007) provides a set of research-based principles for curriculum provision:

> Provide regular challenges to high-ability and gifted students in their area(s) of talent development.

> Give them regular opportunities to learn independently in their areas of passion and talent.

> Provide them with various forms of subject-based and year-level acceleration.

> Provide opportunities for them to socialise and to learn with like-ability peers.

> For specific curriculum areas, differentiate teaching in pace, amount of review and practice, and organisation of content presentation.

Acceleration includes:

> locating the student in a higher year for more advanced teaching
> teaching at the student's rate of learning
> modifying or 'compacting' the curriculum
> a withdrawal program that teaches other topics
> credentialing the gifted student's advanced knowledge
> the student entering school or university at an earlier age
> the student learning more complex and advanced knowledge.

Meta-analyses suggest that acceleration is effective for some gifted students. There are guidelines for deciding whether a high-ability or gifted student is suitable for accelerated progression.

To differentiate the content or curriculum, teachers can:

> plan more advanced levels of understanding of a topic; these are the differentiated knowledge goals
> plan the learning program to achieve these higher-level outcomes.

To plan the learning program, teachers decide:

> the knowledge pathway
> how to identify the students who have the existing knowledge needed to engage in the project
> the challenges or provocations to engage students in the project
> the necessary information sources and learning activities

> how to guide students to create and evaluate their personal intuitive theories of action
> the contexts in which the students will learn
> how to group students to learn throughout the project
> how to support students to learn independently
> how to guide students to monitor regularly what they have learnt
> how students will display their understanding
> how to assess students' responses to the differentiated curriculum unit
> how these students will use their understanding of a topic to enhance peer group knowledge.

References

Assouline SG, Colangelo N, Lupkowski-Shoplik A, Lipscomb J and Forstad L (2009) *Iowa Acceleration Scale*, Great Potential Press, Tucson, AZ.

Assouline SG, Colangelo N, VanTassel-Baska J and Lupkowski-Shoplik A (2015) *A nation empowered: evidence trumps the excuses holding back America's brightest students (Vol. 2)*, Belin-Blank Center, Iowa City, IA, accessed 1 November 2023. http://www.accelerationinstitute.org/Nation_Empowered/Order/NationEmpowered_Vol2.pdf

Betts G, Kapushion B, and Carey RJ (2016) 'The autonomous learner model: supporting the development of problem finders, creative problem solvers, and producers of knowledge to successfully navigate the 21st Century', in Ambrose D and Sternberg RJ (eds) *Giftedness and talent in the 21st century. Adapting to the turbulence of globalization* (Vol. 10), Sense Publishers, Rotterdam, The Netherlands.

Board of Studies NSW (2000) *The guidelines for accelerated progression, revised 2000*, Board of Studies NSW, Sydney.

Chandra Handa M (2019) 'Leading differentiated learning for the gifted', *Roeper Review*, 41(2):102–118, doi:10.1080/02783193.2019.1585213.

Colangelo N, Assouline SG and Gross MU (2004) *A nation deceived: how schools hold back America's brightest students. The Templeton national report on acceleration. Volumes 1 and 2*, Connie Belin & Jacqueline N. Blank International Center for Gifted Education and Talent Development, Iowa City, IA.

De Bono E (1982) *De Bono's thinking course*, BBC Books.

Feldhusen JF, Proctor TB and Black KN (1986) 'Guidelines for grade advancement of precocious children', *Roeper Review*, 9(1):25–27, doi:10.1080/02783198609553000.

Gelgoot ES, Bulakowski PF and Worrell F (2020) 'Flipping a classroom for academically talented students', *Journal of Advanced Academics*, 31(4):451–469, doi:10.1177/1932202X20919357.

Kim M (2016) 'A meta-analysis of the effects of enrichment programs on gifted students', *Gifted Child Quarterly*, 60(2):102–116, doi:10.1177/0016986216630607.

Kivunja C (2015) 'Using De Bono's six thinking hats model to teach critical thinking and problem solving skills essential for success in the 21st century economy', *Creative Education*, 6(03):380–391, doi:10.4236/ce.2015.63037.

Lubinski D and Benbow CP (2000) 'States of excellence', *American Psychologist*, 55(1):137–150, doi:10.1037/0003-066X.55.1.137.

McCann MT (2003) *A study of visual intelligence and the influence of a visual enrichment program on measures of IQ and creativity on 10 and 11 year-old students nominated as gifted* [doctoral dissertation], Graduate School of Education Faculty of the Professions University of Adelaide, accessed 1 November 2023. https://digital.library.adelaide.edu.au/dspace/bitstream/2440/101507/2/01front.pdf

Olszewski-Kubilius P and Lee SY (2004) 'The role of participation in in-school and outside-of-school activities in the talent development of gifted students', *Journal of Secondary Gifted Education*, 15(3):107–123, doi:10.4219/jsge-2004-454.

Potts JA and Potts S (2017) 'Is your gifted child ready for online learning?', *Gifted Child Today*, 40(4):226–231, doi:10.1177/1076217517722182.

Renzulli JS and Renzulli SR (2010) 'The schoolwide enrichment model: a focus on student strengths and interests', *Gifted Education International*, 26(2–3):140–156, doi.org/10.1177/026142941002600303.

Rogers KB (2007) 'Lessons learned about educating the gifted and talented: a synthesis of the research on educational practice', *Gifted Child Quarterly*, 51(4):382–396, doi:10.1177/0016986207306324.

Rogers KB (2015) 'The academic, socialization, and psychological effects of acceleration: research synthesis', in Assouline SG, Colangelo N, VanTassel-Baska J and Lupkowski-Shoplik A (eds) *A nation empowered: evidence trumps the excuses holding back America's brightest students (Vol. 2)*, Belin-Blank Center, Iowa City, IA, accessed 1 November 2023. http://www.accelerationinstitute.org/Nation_Empowered/Order/NationEmpowered_Vol2.pdf

Sanderson E and Greenberger R (2011) 'Evaluating online programs through a gifted lens', *Gifted Child Today*, 34(3):42–55, doi:10.1177/107621751103400311.

Steenbergen-Hu S and Moon SM (2011) 'The effects of acceleration on high-ability learners: a meta-analysis', *Gifted Child Quarterly*, 55(1):39–53, doi:10.1177/0016986210383155.

Sternberg RJ (1986) 'A triarchic theory of intellectual giftedness', in Sternberg RJ and Davison JE (eds) *Conceptions of giftedness*, Cambridge University Press, Cambridge, MA.

Sukarno FM (2019) 'Improving students' higher order thinking skills through implementing open inquiry-KWHL chart', *International Journal of Science and Research*, 8(4):264–267, doi:10.21275/ART20196715.

Swan B, Coulombe-Quach XL, Huang A, Godek J, Becker D and Zhou Y (2015) 'Meeting the needs of gifted and talented students: case study of a virtual learning lab in a rural middle school', *Journal of Advanced Academics*, 26(4):294–319, doi.org/10.1177/1932202X15603366.

Thomson D (2011) 'Conversations with teachers on the benefits and challenges of online learning for gifted students', *Gifted Child Today*, 34(3):31–39, doi:10.1177/107621751103400309.

Tomlinson CA and Moon TR (2013) *Assessment and student success in a differentiated classroom*, ASCD.

Vaughn VL, Feldhusen JF and Asher JW (1991) 'Meta-analyses and review of research o pull-out programs in gifted education', *Gifted Child Quarterly*, 35(2):92–98, doi:10.1177/001698629103500208.

CHAPTER 9

How to differentiate regular classroom teaching to foster high-level outcomes

Introduction

Chapter 8 described how to differentiate the curriculum to achieve high-level outcomes and noted the 5 components of educational provision that models of differentiation recommend adjusting. This chapter describes how to modify or differentiate the teaching during a session to accommodate the learning profiles of high-ability and gifted students and to scaffold and support how these students learn. The focus here is on high-ability and gifted differentiation for the regular classroom, although it can also be applied in the accelerated context and can also benefit regular students, as the scaffolding helps them form their interpretations.

The main ideas in this chapter are shown in Figure 9.1.

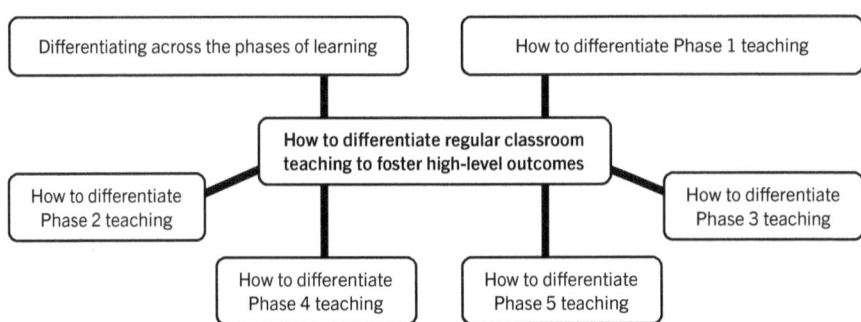

Figure 9.1. Differentiating regular classroom teaching to foster high-level outcomes

Differentiating teaching

This differentiation is intended to challenge or 'provoke' students to think about and interpret the teaching information in open-ended ways that extend it and to link ideas in more complex ways. High-ability and gifted students can then form higher level understanding and intuitive theories of action about the teaching, which lead to advanced outcomes. Regular teaching without the challenges or 'provocations' is less likely to guide high-ability and gifted students to realise high-level outcomes.

Students with high-ability or gifted learning profiles differ in how they use thinking strategies. Some use them spontaneously and the teaching focuses and validates their thinking activity. Others can use thinking strategies but don't do so automatically; the teaching directs and guides their activity. Reviews of the effectiveness of differentiation across disciplines and year levels (García-Martínez et al. 2021; Heacox and Cash 2020; Scott 2023; Tomlinson 2017; VanTassel-Baska and Baska 2021) note the importance of using students' learning profiles to design teaching provision.

It has been noted internationally that although teachers are aware of the need to differentiate for high-ability and gifted students, they are less likely to practise it in their teaching (Caldwell 2012; Kilgore 2018; VanTassel-Baska et al. 2021). Leaders and teachers differ in how they perceive differentiated teaching practices; for example, what these practices 'look like' and their frequency (Handra Chandra 2019). There is a need for ongoing professional education that targets teaching procedures used in classrooms. VanTassel-Baska et al. (2020, 2021) developed the Classroom Observation Scale-Revised (COS-R), based on best practice in gifted education internationally, to monitor these teaching procedures.

This chapter builds on VanTassel-Baska et al.'s (2020) recommendations. It describes how teachers can scaffold students to learn the content in advanced ways and describes a framework for differentiating teaching across the phases of knowledge enhancement during learning. The description can also equip leaders to understand and monitor differentiation practice in their school and to know what a typical differentiated teaching session might 'look like'.

Differentiating across the phases of learning

Successful learning can be viewed as proceeding through the 5 'phases' of knowledge change, shown in Figure 9.2.

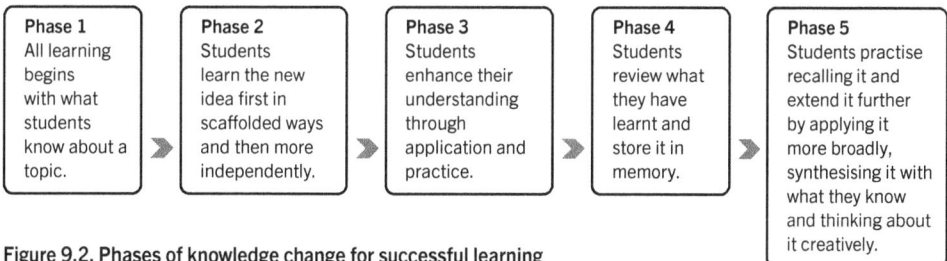

Figure 9.2. Phases of knowledge change for successful learning

It is recommended that differentiated teaching be aligned with this learning sequence. For students with high-ability or gifted learning profiles, the 5 phases can be differentiated as shown in Figure 9.3.

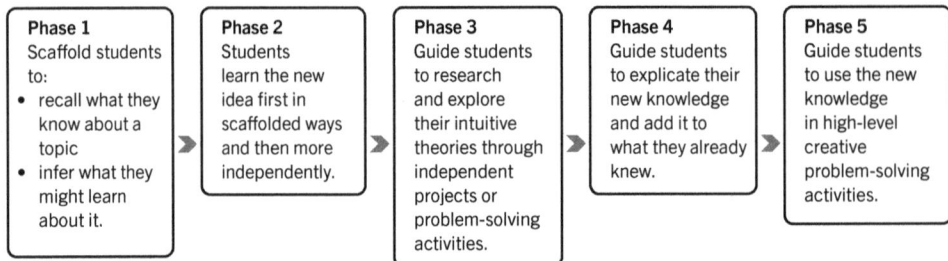

Figure 9.3 Suggested phases of learning for high-ability profiles

At each phase of the learning-teaching sequence, teachers can use various types of questions to challenge and scaffold students' knowledge and thinking. These are shown in Table 9.1. The questions increase in their complexity and lead to intuitive theories of action. They can be used to teach any topic in deeper, more complex ways.

Table 9.1. Ways to challenge and scaffold students' thinking

THINKING	EXAMPLES	QUESTIONS
Infer patterns in the ideas	• Extend a pattern, summarise, generalise across contexts. • Infer or predict patterns, ideas or possibilities not mentioned in teaching. • Make far transfer links, use analogies. • Identify what specific ideas or contexts share. • Visualise ideas changing, create new ideas.	• What do these instances or contexts have in common? • What is the pattern here? • What might happen if …?
Infer possible trends	• Link 2 or more patterns in possible causal or consequential relationships. • Analyse new ideas from multiple perspectives. • Evaluate ideas in terms of their consequences and implications. • Think creatively and flexibly, pursue originality and novel outcomes.	• How/why did the trend affect the pattern? • How did the patterns affect …? • 'If this happens, then …, but because of … I would …'. • What if …?

Synthesise generalities and rules	• Synthesise inferred patterns into rules and general propositions. • Identify boundaries of an idea. • Analyse and/or evaluate rules and principles.	• Replace the main idea or topic with another plausible main idea. How does the interpretation change? • What is the rule here?
Infer ethical issues	• Link moral or ethical issues with the rules or general propositions.	• What/how/why should/might …?
Infer, synthesise big ideas	• Synthesise rules and principles into big ideas. • Infer the main or big ideas in the intuitive theories. • Infer and investigate the implications and possibilities of 'big ideas'. • Infer how the 'big ideas' could be used to solve problems, make decisions and generate creative outcomes.	• What do you think could be the big idea here? • How can you use your new knowledge in creative, novel ways? 'If this happens, then … , but because of … I would …'. • What might you do if … Why wouldn't you …? What if …?'

These questions invite students to reflect on their interpretations of the teaching in open-ended, divergent ways. You can apply this sequence to any topic to:

> differentiate your teaching at each phase as you guide and lead student thinking, and to understand students' interpretations of the teaching at each phase

> plan higher levels of understanding of a topic for the gifted students to research and study (as discussed in Chapter 8)

> ensure that the classroom climate and organisation support and foster students' use of these ways of knowing and thinking.

The following sections describe how to differentiate teaching for students with high-ability and gifted learning profiles at each phase of learning and teaching.

How to differentiate Phase 1 teaching: what students already know

This phase stimulates students' existing knowledge of the topic at the beginning of a teaching session. The types of tasks to probe students' existing knowledge and thinking about the topic are shown in Table 9.2. These tasks ask students to infer in various ways about the topic. The tasks will indicate those students who can form a higher level understanding of the topic.

Table 9.2. Tasks that probe students' existing knowledge

STUDENT ACTIVITY	PRE-TEACHING IDENTIFICATION TASKS
Infer mental images of the topic	Ask students to describe the images they form when they hear the topic or see imagery of it. They can: • talk about the images and unpack the context and any narrative they create about the images • draw pictures that show their ideas about the topic • make a physical model of the ideas • act out their thinking.
Suggest vocabulary for the topic	Students can: • infer and list words that might be used to develop the topic • suggest synonyms and antonyms for key concepts in the topic • select the key concepts for a topic from a list • select key pictures for a topic • label a diagram about the topic.
Recall what they know about the topic or subject	Invite students to: • tell you all they know about a topic • 'take you on a journey' through what they know and believe about the topic • elaborate and develop what they report • answer questions, including inferential questions about the topic.

Make far transfer, fluid analogy	Ask students to: • name other topics they think of when they hear the topic • say what the topic reminds them of.
Ask questions regarding the topic	Ask students to: • suggest questions the topic might answer for them or questions they might be able to answer having learnt the topic • suggest inferential questions: How might …?, What could happen if …?, When should …?, How could you tell if …?
Show how they organise concepts	Ask students to: • link key ideas of the topic visually in concept maps or flow charts; for example, 'Here are some words from the topic. Draw a concept map that shows how you think they are linked: breathe, blood, cell, vessels, oxygen, lungs, cough, windpipe.'
Say the thinking strategies they will use	Invite students to: • say what they will do to learn • tell you how they will plan for it • learn or solve a task.

The teaching here scaffolds students to apply their inferential, analytic, evaluative and synthesis skills to their existing knowledge of a topic. The tasks do not restrict their thinking; they are intended to show the breadth and depth of a student's knowledge of the topic. The climate is differentiated to encourage open-ended responses. Using both verbal and imagery contexts accommodates multiple high-ability and gifted profiles.

How to differentiate Phase 2 teaching: learning new ideas

Phase 2 teaching is when students begin learning the new content. Teaching can be differentiated by adding prompts and questions that elicit higher order thinking by applying the types of thinking presented in the first column of Table 9.1 (see p. 158). The teaching asks students to infer, think divergently and analyse their emerging new understanding, to look for patterns and principles and to synthesise and evaluate the ideas.

Two examples of differentiating teaching are shown in Table 9.3 and 9.4. The first topic teaches the structure of the hand. Students see an X-ray photo of a human hand and learn that each finger has 3 bones, the thumb has 2 bones and the palm has 13 bones. The second example involves students reading Chapter 2 of *Boy* by Roald Dahl. Each teaching session begins with a challenge. Its purpose is to provide a focus for the students' learning and to motivate engagement, curiosity and thinking. Each question asks the students to think inferentially, analytically and synthetically about their interpretations. You can generate similar probes for any topic you teach.

Table 9.3 Differentiated teaching: the structure of the hand

THINKING	QUESTIONS
Challenge	• How do you think the bones in each finger are joined together so that they can move?
Infer patterns in the ideas	• Why do you think the joints in the finger bones are curved? • Why might the thumb bones be separate from the finger bones? • How many bones do you think are in each of your toes? How did you decide?
Infer possible trends	• What do joints in our fingers and thumb allow us to do? If we had only one bone in our fingers, how could a finger move? • Move your thumb. How does it move differently from the fingers? How can you tell it has 2 bones? • Suppose you design a 'robot' hand. How would the number of joints in each of its 'fingers' affect what it could do?
Synthesise generalities and rules	• How could you tell which pawed animals in a zoo might have 2 or more bones in each digit? • What if the base of the thumb bone were closer to the base for the finger bones? How well could your thumb move? • Do you think the bones in your big toes are more like the bones in your thumb or the bones in your fingers?
Infer ethical issues	• How has the development of the human hand helped people in history?

Table 9.3 continued

Infer, synthesise big ideas	• How and why do you think human hands have changed over history? • How would our lives be different if we had fewer bones in each hand? • How might our hands change in the future as we use them differently? • How could medical discoveries help us use our hands differently?

Table 9.4 Differentiated teaching: Chapter 2 of *Boy* by Roald Dahl

THINKING	QUESTIONS
Challenge	• This chapter is about Roald's time in primary school. What might have been important to him during this time?
Infer patterns in the ideas	• Why do you think Roald Dahl thought the licorice bootlaces were the best value? • What does Thwaites' story about licorice tell you about the boys? • Why do you think Roald Dahl described his favourite sweets in such detail?
Infer possible trends	• Why do you think Roald Dahl describes Mrs Pratchett in the way that he does? • What feelings do you think the boys had as they passed the sweet shop? • What do their actions tell us about how they felt? • What might they have said to themselves?
Synthesise generalities and rules	• How does the author use language to tell us how the boys felt? • Roald Dahl says: 'To us it was what a bar is to a drunk or a church is to a Bishop.' Why do you think he says this? • The next sentence begins with 'But'. Why do you think Roald Dahl used but in this case?
Infer ethical issues	• How would the boys' ethics and morals clash with those of Mrs Pratchett?
Infer, synthesise big ideas	• What do we know about Roald Dahl from this chapter? • What do you think is the purpose of this chapter in *Boy*? How does it fit with Chapter 1? • What do you think Roald Dahl might think of young boys being sent to boarding school?

Differentiation at Phase 2 scaffolds the high-ability and gifted students to form more sophisticated understandings of a topic. They use their thinking to form more complex relationships, which then become part of their intuitive theories about the topic. The thinking leads them to generate possibilities about it. In Phase 3, they target explicitly more advanced content about the topic.

How to differentiate Phase 3 teaching: application and practice

Phase 3 of the teaching can focus more explicitly on curriculum differentiation for high-ability and gifted students. These students usually learn a topic faster than their regular peers. While their peers follow the regular curriculum and practise and apply the ideas taught at Phase 2, high-ability and gifted students can pursue more advanced curriculum goals by teachers implementing the 12-step learning program described in Chapter 8 (see pp. 136–141).

High-ability students can work through tasks that guide them to manipulate the concepts in greater breadth and depth and to synthesise more complex concepts. They form a more complex and sophisticated understanding of a topic, organise and integrate the ideas in novel ways and generate their intuitive theories. These lead to high-level outcomes.

The modified learning pathway combines teacher-directed activity and autonomous self-directed learning by the students. It can include an investigative project and complex problem-solving, and outcomes can be shared with peers.

Teachers can also scaffold these students how to research, analyse, evaluate and rationalise their intuitive theories in open-ended ways, modify them if necessary and convert them to logical theories.

How to differentiate Phase 4 teaching: review and store

Effective teaching generally scaffolds students to review what they have learnt and to store the new knowledge in long-term memory. Differentiation for high-ability and gifted students scaffolds them to:

> review and consolidate what they have learnt. Students select and integrate the main ideas, subordinate ideas and details and integrate them into an intuitive theory of action. They identify what they know and believe could be possible now and how their skill or knowledge has changed

> link the new ideas with what they already knew. Students identify how the new ideas fit with and extend what they already knew. They communicate the questions they can answer now and the types of problems the new ideas allow them to deal with or solve

> review what they have learnt about how to learn. Students identify the thinking actions they used and suggest how they might use the thinking in the future

> review what they have learnt about themselves as a learner.

How to differentiate Phase 5 teaching: recall and apply new ideas broadly

Effective teaching frequently scaffolds students to recall, chunk and automatise the new ideas. High-ability students can use their knowledge faster and more broadly; it has the characteristics of 'expertise' (Ericsson et al. 2007).

Phase 5 differentiation for high-ability and gifted students scaffolds them to:

> reorganise their understanding, chunk it into larger units and form a synthesised 'big idea' understanding, scaffolding them to analyse and evaluate new ideas from multiple perspectives

> think creatively using the ideas and form possibilities and options about them

> think about the ideas affectively and aesthetically, appreciate them and see 'beauty' in them

> prepare or organise their knowledge so that they can display and share it for assessment purposes.

High-ability students link their 'big idea' understanding with values and attitudes in particular cultural contexts and use it to solve social and cultural problems; this has been described as 'diffuse social' problem-solving (Hedlund et al. 2006; Munro 2019). In his model of successful intelligence, Sternberg (2010) describes this linking as 'wisdom' and gifted knowledge as a synthesis of intelligence, creativity and wisdom.

Online teaching and differentiation

The online teaching format offers a valuable learning context for high-ability and gifted students. The teaching information at any time can be structured to take account of what the student knows and how they are thinking. It can take account of their ability to think inductively and inferentially and to form intuitive theories.

Online teaching works

Differentiated online teaching has been used to improve high-ability and gifted students' use of a range of thinking skills: inquiry, problem-solving, critical thinking and self-regulating skills (Periathiruvadi and Rinn 2012; Potts 2019). The contexts are often open-ended activities such as problem-based learning in domains including mathematics, science and humanities. Students learning in these contexts are usually more positive about what they've learnt and more motivated and able to share their new understanding.

Online differentiated teaching can provide a valuable learning opportunity for twice-exceptional students. It can be modified to include multimodal information sources for those students who are challenged by literacy demands and can provide alternative social learning contexts for those with psychological challenges. It can also provide appropriate learning materials for students in rural or isolated contexts, so long as they have reliable internet access.

Assistance to modify online teaching

The 'differentiation adjustment tool' provided at the NSW Department of Education (NSW Department of Education n.d.) as part of its High Potential and Gifted Education provision is useful for schools wanting either to develop their own online teaching content or to differentiate and modify existing online content. It describes procedures for differentiating teaching to adjust:

> - the complexity of the students' understanding
> - the challenge of the learning activities
> - the choices in the learning activities
> - the level of abstraction in the students' understanding
> - the use of creative, critical and higher order thinking during the learning activities
> - the pace of teaching
> - the authenticity of the content
> - the learning environment.

Online teaching can scaffold high-ability and gifted students to form a more sophisticated understanding and knowledge (Periathiruvadi and Rinn 2012; Potts 2019).

What your school can do now

This chapter recommends ways in which the regular teaching practice can be 'fine-tuned' to foster high-level outcomes. Professional learning activities to enhance this aspect of your school's provision include those presented here.

Evaluate current differentiation of teaching

Invite teachers to evaluate the extent to which they currently differentiate their teaching systematically. The 5-phase knowledge change process provides a systematic framework for evaluating current provision for each high-ability and gifted learning profile. To what extent is differentiation at each phase currently implemented?

Evaluate questions and tasks

Invite teachers to analyse and evaluate the questions, tasks and differentiated teaching examples presented in Tables 9.1 to 9.3 of this chapter and identify the types of student thinking they are intended to stimulate. Teachers can unpack the ways in which these questions are asking students to act on and think about their understanding. Have them suggest possible responses the students may provide to the questions.

Identify how differentiation can be improved

From their evaluation of their current practices, you can invite teachers to identify how differentiation in their classroom practices could be improved. The 5-phase knowledge change process again provides a framework for this.

Develop a professional learning agenda

Use staff responses to the 2 preceding evaluations in this section to identify a professional agenda that enhances staff skill to implement differentiation at each phase of teaching. Teachers can plan the prompts and cues they will add to their teaching to scaffold high-ability and gifted thinking and understanding. They can share and evaluate their recommended differentiations and adjust them where necessary. Workshops can teach staff how to develop the specific cues, to plan and implement the differentiated teaching and to interpret student responses.

Plan an implementation agenda

You can use the Classroom Observation Scale-Revised (VanTassel-Baska et al. 2021) described earlier (see p. 157) to monitor and evaluate the differentiated teaching procedures each teacher is using. Staff can also use it to plan and improve their own provision. Collaborative planning and teaching, group analysis and evaluation of recordings of differentiated teaching scenarios contribute substantially to professional learning and to creative teaching options.

Summary

Teaching in the regular classroom and in advanced teaching contexts can be differentiated to include provocations that challenge high-ability and gifted students to form higher level understanding or intuitive theories of action and scaffold the students to interpret the teaching information in more complex, open-ended ways.

The differentiation can be implemented at each of the 5 phases of learning and teaching:

> - At phase 1 students are scaffolded to recall what they know about a topic and to infer what they might learn about it.
>
> - At phase 2 they are scaffolded to form intuitive theories about the teaching by challenging them to think about it in various ways.
>
> - At phase 3 they are guided to research and explore their intuitive theories through independent projects or problem-solving activities.
>
> - At phase 4 they are guided to explicate their new knowledge and add it to what they already knew.
>
> - At phase 5 they are guided to use the new knowledge in high-level creative problem-solving activities.

Teachers can use the questions and cues described in this chapter to challenge and scaffold students' knowledge and thinking at each phase, on any topic. These cues invite students to reflect on their interpretations of the teaching in open-ended, divergent ways.

References

Caldwell DW (2012) 'Educating gifted students in the regular classroom: efficacy, attitudes, and differentiation of instruction', *Electronic Theses and Dissertations*, 822, accessed 14 March 2024. https://digitalcommons.georgiasouthern.edu/etd/822

Chandra Handa M (2019) 'Leading differentiated learning for the gifted', *Roeper Review*, 41(2):102–118, doi:10.1080/02783193.2019.1585213.

Ericsson KA, Roring RW and Nandagopa K (2007) 'Giftedness and evidence for reproducibly superior performance: an account based on the expert performance framework', *High Ability Studies*, 18(1), 3–56, doi:10.1080/13598130701350593.

García-Martínez I, Gutiérrez Cáceres R, Luque de la Rosa A and León SP (2021) 'Analysing educational interventions with gifted students', Systematic Review, *Children (Basel, Switzerland)*, 8(5):365, doi:10.3390/children8050365.

Heacox D and Cash RM (2020) *Differentiation for gifted learners: going beyond the basics*, Free Spirit Publishing.

Hedlund J, Wilt JM, Nebel KL, Ashford SJ and Sternberg RJ (2006) 'Assessing practical intelligence in business school admissions: a supplement to the graduate management admissions test', *Learning and Individual Differences*, 16(2):101–127, doi:10.1016/j.lindif.2005.07.005.

Kilgore KA (2018) *Teacher perspectives on differentiation for gifted students in the general education classroom*, Walden Dissertations and Doctoral Studies, 5488, accessed 8 May 2024. https://scholarworks.waldenu.edu/dissertations/5488.

Munro J (2019) 'Identifying gifted learning in the regular classroom: seeking intuitive theories', in Smith SR (ed) *Springer international handbook of giftedness & talent development in the Asia-Pacific*, Springer Nature Singapore Pty Ltd., Gateway East, Singapore, doi:10.1007/978-981-13-3021-6_22-1.

NSW Department of Education (n.d.) *High Potential and Gifted Education*, NSW Government Education website, accessed 14 March 2024. https://education.nsw.gov.au/teaching-and-learning/high-potential-and-gifted-education

Periathiruvadi S and Rinn AN (2012) 'Technology in gifted education: a review of best practices and empirical research', *Journal of Research on Technology in Education*, 45(2):153–169.

Potts JA (2019) 'Profoundly gifted students' perceptions of virtual classrooms', *Gifted Child Quarterly*, 63(1):58–80, doi:10.1177/0016986218801075.

Scott K (2023) 'Differentiation for today's gifted learners', in Scott K (ed) *Strategies and considerations for educating the academically gifted*, IGI Global, Hershey, PA, doi:10.4018/978-1-6684-6677-3.ch004.

Sternberg RJ (2010) 'WICS: a new model for school psychology', *School Psychology International,* 31:599–616, doi:10.1177/0143034310386534.

Tomlinson CA (2017) 'Differentiated instruction', in *Fundamentals of gifted education: considering multiple perspectives*, Routledge.

VanTassel-Baska J and Baska A (2021) *Curriculum planning and instructional design for gifted learners*, 2nd edn, Routledge, doi:10.4324/9781003234050-2.

VanTassel-Baska J, Hubbard GH and Robbins J (2020) 'Differentiation of instruction for gifted learners: collated evaluative studies of teacher classroom practices', *Roeper Review*, 42(3), doi:10.1080/02783193.2020.1765919.

VanTassel-Baska J, Hubbard GF and Robbins JI (2021) 'Differentiation of instruction for gifted learners: collated evaluative studies of teacher classroom practices', in Smith SR (ed) *Handbook of giftedness and talent development in the Asia-Pacific,* Springer Nature Singapore Pty Ltd., Gateway East, Singapore.

CHAPTER 10

How to differentiate classroom culture and climate to achieve high-level outcomes

Introduction

Many students with high learning ability do not achieve high-level outcomes in the classroom. Some report being bored with classroom learning or disengage from it. Some report feeling different from or rejected by their peers or feel they aren't free to display what they 'really' think or believe. These feelings and the reduced likelihood of high-level outcomes are due in part to the culture and climate of the classroom. This is likely to change only when the culture or climate are modified to take account of how high-ability and gifted students learn.

A culture is formed by a group of individuals who share a set of values and common goals. It values specific knowledge, ways of thinking and communicating, and actions to achieve its goals. Each classroom is a culture. It is a learning space that values particular ways of learning and interacting. Each student forms beliefs about what it means to be a student and a teacher, how each role works and what are reasonable expectations. They learn, for example, how well they can trust their teacher and themselves when learning.

Chapter 8 noted the 5 components of educational provision that models of differentiation recommend adjusting. This chapter focuses on differentiating the classroom climate and culture to scaffold and support how high-ability and gifted students learn.

The main ideas in this chapter are shown in Figure 10.1.

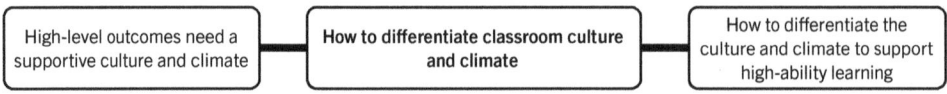

Figure 10.1. Differentiating classroom culture and climate

High-level outcomes need a supportive culture and climate

High-level outcomes are achieved via environmental interactions

Factors such as cultural opportunity, values and support influence the achievement of advanced learning outcomes. The role of the learning environment generally in developing talent or high-level outcomes has been increasingly recognised over the past 2 decades.

High ability or aptitude by itself is not sufficient for high-level outcomes. Ziegler and Stoeger (2019:130) describe talent development in terms of the student interacting with their material, social and informational environments, and Gagné (2020) refers to the environmental factors for talent development as 'catalysts'.

Classroom cultures that foster high-level and talented outcomes show positive attitudes to learning and education, offer opportunities for one-on-one learning, such as mentoring or individual coaching, encourage students to set and pursue short-term and long-term goals for learning and achieving excellence in a talent domain, minimise distractions to self-directed learning activity and allocate sufficient time for this (Ziegler et al. 2017). They also provide the opportunity for students to explore how their advanced learning activity can be applied in a range of contexts and how the specific contexts affect the learning outcomes.

Being able to see opportunities for interactions in an environment or context, that is, its 'affordances' (APA 2023), has been unpacked in talent development in sport (Rothwell et al. 2022) and in creativity (Glaveanu 2015). These perspectives show how high-level outcomes for any topic gradually emerge as the students interact with aspects of the environment in which teaching is implemented.

The classroom is a culture

An appropriate classroom climate and culture that scaffolds students to use their high ability and giftedness to generate high-level outcomes is necessary. The culture validates and supports the high-ability and gifted thinking and offers opportunities for students to display their advanced understanding.

The classroom climate refers to the interactions it values and encourages as ways of 'being a learner and a thinker'. The culture is tacit or invisible and is communicated through teachers' interactions with their students and what teachers show they value and expect through their practices. It can let students know that intuitive theories of action are expected and valued.

Alternatively, a classroom culture can cause students to hide their higher understanding and knowing. They avoid sharing their understanding because they don't know how the culture will respond to it. Teachers need to provide the climate, culture and organisation that support the emergence of high-level outcomes. This includes making formative assessment decisions about what and how to teach next.

The classroom culture and climate are important for twice-exceptional students. Chapter 5 noted that twice exceptionality can be caused in part by the classroom culture not accommodating or supporting how these students learn. It can restrict or be a barrier to learning for them. Teachers may need to know how to differentiate the culture and climate so that they align more closely with the cultural diversity of some students. This may include providing appropriate cultural support and resources.

Classroom cultures differ in how they value, tolerate and respect diversity and difference. Some average learning students in mixed ability classrooms perceive students who have high-ability and gifted learning profiles as 'different'. Some educators associate giftedness with elitism. High-ability and gifted students in these cultures can sometimes experience negative valuing. This can lead to negative social consequences for them, including feeling stigmatised, alienated, excluded from functional social interactions and being the target of ostracism or bullying.

These consequences can lead to these students withdrawing from participating in regular classroom activities or attempting to hide or mask their high-ability and gifted thinking and high-level outcomes. They can also impact on the students' overall sense of wellbeing, their self-identify and self-valuing. Students can experience the classroom as threatening and can display negative emotional responses, which are described in more detail in Chapter 11.

Educators need to be aware of and sensitive to these possibilities and the extent to which the classroom culture and climate can influence them. They also need to reflect on ways of maintaining inclusive and supportive cultures.

How to differentiate the culture and climate

How can the culture and climate that support regular students' learning be differentiated to support the effective learning of high-ability and gifted students? The earlier chapters have unpacked the learning characteristics that the culture and climate need to support, such as the opportunity for self-directed learning towards advanced knowledge. High-ability and gifted students are less likely to achieve high-level or talented outcomes without an appropriately differentiated culture and climate that supports their learning activity. A differentiated culture and climate for high-ability and gifted students has the following characteristics.

It values and respects students' existing knowledge and thinking

A climate and culture that is differentiated values and respects students' existing knowledge and thinking, as well as a range of ways of knowing and is open, accepting and non-judgemental. Students are encouraged at any time to recognise and value all they know and to share their knowledge, including unusual or unexpected interpretations, in a variety of ways.

Students' knowledge and thinking are also valued and respected by a culture and climate that:

> - provides the opportunity for independent, self-directed and intrinsically motivated learning; students are encouraged to be active participants in learning, using their self-teaching abilities to explore ideas, take risks and balance these with being programmed externally; they collaborate with teachers to set personal daily and weekly work goals and to develop skills to manage their learning
> - encourages students to pursue knowledge in open-ended ways and to set personal goals
> - communicates high expectations, shows a valuing of effort and the belief that learning is open-ended and means changing what one knows
> - uses pre-assessment to identify students' existing knowledge and skills and to compact the curriculum for students who have already mastered the core
> - uses assessment and learning tasks that allow students to show all they know in a range of ways, including expressing their inferential and creative thinking about a topic and through multimodal activities like drawing, acting ideas out or making models; particularly for students who are twice exceptional.

It accommodates multiple high-ability and gifted learning profiles

A differentiated culture and climate takes account of students with multiple high-ability and gifted learning profiles. For example, it considers those with imagery and performance high-ability and gifted profiles, allowing them to learn in imagery–spatial and practical contexts through hands-on activities and to show mechanical or technological creativity. It teaches them to say their imagery and action understanding. Some students need to convert the imagery or action understanding to a verbal form so that they can talk about it. A culture and climate that is differentiated permits high-ability and gifted students to learn in multiple ways; for example, to learn in 'big jumps' and in a step-wise way, to infer in directions away from the teaching and to raise ideas that challenge it.

Multiple high-ability and gifted learning profiles are also accommodated by a culture and climate that:

> explicitly communicates the criteria for success

> offers differentiated classroom processes and structures and uses flexible classroom organisation; for example, various grouping options to allow work with like-minded peers and with mentors through virtual interaction

> uses collaborative and cooperative learning contexts, such as 'jigsaw' and think–pair–share, and learning centres with activities that vary in complexity and foster learning in a range of contexts (Neber et al. 2001)

> provides appropriately differentiated teaching and curriculum opportunities, such as enrichment and accelerated pace, to allow independent study on student interest

> provides a range of resources to support individual investigation and interests, including information sources and access to mentoring

> takes account of social and emotional issues often associated with high-ability and gifted learning

> scaffolds students to improve their social competence awareness and skill and to learn acceptable social behaviours and conventions and uses a range of positive emotions in the classroom, such as humour and optimism, to develop rapport; this can include helping students improve how they share knowledge with peers

> deals positively with the cognitive stress and anxiety high-ability and gifted students often experience.

Each of these factors is demonstrated in teaching behaviours in a classroom. This includes the formative feedback teachers give and the student responses they value explicitly. High-ability students need to perceive that the classroom culture and climate support, value and respect their interpretations of the teaching. When these factors are explicit in a classroom culture and climate, high-level outcomes are more likely to emerge.

Online learning and differentiating the classroom culture and climate

Online learning offers a supportive differentiated learning culture and environment that may be valued by younger and older high-ability and gifted students (Gilson and Lee 2023; McKoy and Merry 2023). It achieves all of the outcomes listed in the previous section. It fosters critical thinking, reflection and problem-solving skills, in part by collaborating with other high-ability and gifted peers in multimodal ways using online discussion forums, and provides the opportunity for high-ability and gifted students to learn independently.

Online learning can foster interest in the content, particularly for younger students. It can also offer flexibility and the opportunity for students to learn at their own pace and can provide access to content that is not available in regular classes. High-ability and gifted students also value the social aspects of the online culture that permit them to interact with like-minded peers and to share ideas and opinions more openly (Gilson and Lee 2023; McKoy and Merry 2023).

What your school can do now

How well does the learning culture and climate in classrooms in your school optimise the likelihood of high-level outcomes? Teachers of high-ability and gifted students need to know how to establish and maintain a culture and climate conducive to this. Some high-ability and gifted students perceive that their understanding and ways of thinking are not valued in the classroom. These students are more likely to be alienated and experience negative emotions. Their identity and self-efficacy as successful learners in the classroom suffer and they are less likely to be intrinsically motivated to set high-level goals.

To enhance your school's provision of an appropriate culture and climate, you can lead staff through a professional development activity that evaluates current provision and identifies an improvement agenda. The activity can identify how classrooms and learning contexts can be differentiated. It is useful for teachers to reflect on and identify what each of the above factors would 'look like' in a classroom.

High-ability students need to perceive that the classroom culture and climate supports, values and respects their interpretations of the teaching. Staff need to be aware that consistent teacher behaviours communicate the culture and climate.

Evaluate current provision

Teachers can examine how well their current provision:

> provides the opportunity for high-ability and gifted students to manage their learning, to learn spontaneously and to display intrinsic motivation to learn

> values and respects students' intuitive theories of action and novel interpretations of the teaching

> provides an appropriate range of learning resources

> fosters students' interest in high-level understanding of topics

> facilitates learning with similar thinking peers and mentors

> helps high-ability and gifted students understand their learning profiles

> helps them improve their peer group social interaction skills.

Identify an improvement agenda

Teachers can identify how they might improve their classroom culture by differentiating it to foster high-level outcomes. It is useful for teachers to:

> reflect on and identify what each of the supportive culture and climate factors would 'look like' in their teaching

> decide the learning culture and climate appropriate for the class, including for those students who have high ability and giftedness

> plan how they will modify aspects of their culture and climate in future teaching and the actions they will take to achieve this

> plan how they will monitor the effectiveness of their culture and climate for supporting high-ability and gifted learning, the data they will collect and how they will modify it if necessary.

Summary

Learning environments and cultures have a significant effect on whether high-ability and gifted students achieve talented or high-level outcomes. Factors include cultural opportunity, values and support.

The climate of the classroom refers to what it values and encourages as ways of 'being a learner and a thinker'. The climate is communicated through a teacher's interactions with their students and what they show they value and expect. It lets students know, for example, whether intuitive theories of action are expected and valued.

The culture and climate that support regular learning can be differentiated to support high-ability and gifted students. A differentiated culture and climate for these students:

- values their existing knowledge and thinking, is open, accepting and non-judgemental and allows them to share their unusual or unexpected interpretations and understanding
- permits them to learn in multiple ways
- balances the opportunity for independent, self-directed and intrinsically motivated learning with structured teaching
- uses pre-assessment to assess students' existing knowledge and skills and to compact the curriculum for students who have mastered the core
- takes account explicitly of students with imagery and performance high-ability and gifted profiles
- uses flexible classroom organisation and permits varied grouping options
- uses assessment and learning tasks that allow students to show all that they know about a topic
- provides appropriately differentiated teaching and curriculum opportunities such as enrichment, curriculum-based pedagogy and accelerated pace to allow independent study
- provides a range of resources to support individual investigation and interests including information sources and access to mentoring
- scaffolds students to improve their social competence awareness and to learn acceptable social behaviours and conventions
- deals positively with the cognitive stress and anxiety these students often experience.

References

APA (American Psychological Association) (2023) *APA dictionary of psychology: affordance*, American Psychological Association website, American Psychological Association, Washington, DC, accessed 2 November 2023. https://dictionary.apa.org/affordance

Gagné F (2020) *Differentiating giftedness from talent: the DMGT perspective on talent development*, Routledge, New York, doi:10.4324/9781003088790

Gilson CM and Lee LE (2023) 'Cultivating a learning environment to support diverse gifted students', *Gifted Child Today*, 46(4):235–249, doi:10.1177/10762175231186454.

Glăveanu VP (2015) 'Creativity as a sociocultural act', *The Journal of Creative Behavior*, 49(3):165–180, doi:10.1002/jocb.94.

McKoy S and Merry KE (2023) 'Engaging advanced learners with differentiated online learning', *Gifted Child Today*, 46(1):48–56, doi:10.1177/10762175221131068.

Neber H, Finsterwald M and Urban N (2001) 'Cooperative learning with gifted and high-achieving students: a review and meta-analyses of 12 studies', *High Ability Studies*, 12(2):199–214, doi:10.1080/13598130120084339.

Rothwell M, Davids K, Woods C, Otte F, Rudd J and Stone J (2022) 'Principles to guide talent development practices in sport: the exemplar case of British rugby league football, *Journal of Expertise*, 5(1):28–37.

Ziegler A, Chandler KL, Vialle W and Stoeger H (2017) 'Exogenous and endogenous learning resources in the Actiotope Model of Giftedness and its significance for gifted education', *Journal for the Education of the Gifted*, 40(4):310–333, doi:10.1177/0162353217734376.

Ziegler A and Stoeger H (2019) 'A nonagonal framework of regulation in talent development (NFRTD)', *High Ability Studies*, 30(1–2):127–145, doi:10.1080/13598139.2019.1598772.

CHAPTER 11

High-ability and gifted students and social–emotional issues

Introduction

Social-emotional issues cover a broad range of overlapping human attributes, including emotions, personality, wellbeing and social interaction skills. They can impact students' overall approach to life and, more specifically, their ability to learn. Educators are better equipped to respond to social-emotional issues when they know what they 'look like', how they impact on learning and how they can be managed. This chapter examines these issues.

To what extent do high-ability and gifted students have unique social-emotional issues that need to be addressed and targeted by schools? What types of issues arise and how can they be resolved? Research examining these questions reports ambiguous findings; some have found that that these students do have particular social-emotional issues, while others have found that they don't (for example, Abdulla Alabbasi et al. 2021; Casino-García et al. 2019; Ogurlu 2021).

The main ideas in this chapter are shown in Figure 11.1.

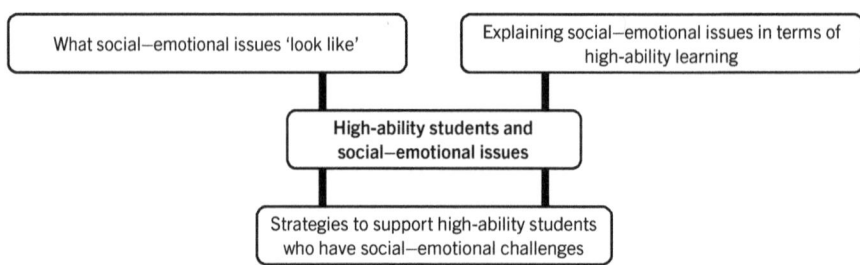

Figure 11.1. High-ability students and social–emotional issues

Social-emotional issues were mentioned briefly in the discussion of twice exceptionality and psychological issues in Chapter 5 (see pp. 59-60). Some students who have a high-ability or gifted learning profile also have an affective disorder, such as oppositional defiant disorder, obsessive compulsive disorder, depression, mood shifts or bipolar, paranoia, chronic anxiety or stress (Foley Nicpon et al. 2010). These issues can be due in part to the students' high learning ability, can mask their high ability and giftedness and can lead to underachievement.

Social-emotional issues vary in their intensity, breadth and impact on students' lives. Responding to them also requires knowledge and skills that differ from those of educators. The issues frequently need to be managed by health and wellbeing professionals, who can unpack and diagnose an issue and plan and implement an intervention. These professionals can recommend the support teachers and schools can provide to assist these students. To provide this support, teachers need to understand what the social-emotional issues 'look like', how they are linked with high-ability and gifted learning and the learning support schools can provide.

What social–emotional issues 'look like'

One way of organising the attributes of social–emotional issues is in terms of the categories of emotional intelligence, moods and 'subjective wellbeing' (Casino-García et al. 2019). Although these categories overlap and interact, for simplicity they will be described here separately.

Moods

Moods are linked with emotions. An emotion is feeling in a particular context, whereas a mood is a more general and longer term affective state; it is the accumulation of feelings over time.

Moods vary in their frequency and their emotional intensity. They are either positive or negative and are affected by an individual's personality and by environmental factors, such as how well a person sees themselves coping in various situations. It is often useful to describe a person's overall mood in terms of the balance between the positive and negative aspects. Positive emotions and moods endure longer and have less impact than negative ones.

Some research reports that high-ability and gifted students have more frequent negative and fewer positive emotions (Casino-García et al. 2019) than their regular learning peers. They are more likely, for example, to feel socially isolated, harassed, anxious, depressed or sad. They often have more intense feelings than their peers about world or life events and show heightened sensitivity and empathy. They show more intense reactions or 'overexcitability' to external and internal stimuli in the sensual, imaginational, intellectual and emotional areas. Some of these students link intense negative emotions with their goals for perfection (Casino-García et al. 2019).

Emotional intelligence

Emotional intelligence (EI) refers to the capacity to perceive, understand and reason about emotions, to regulate and manage them and to use them to facilitate thinking. EI correlates with mood, wellbeing, forming positive social relationships and coping with stress and anxiety. Some research shows that high-ability and gifted students generally display higher scores on assessments of EI than their regular learning peers and that females outperform males (Abdulla Alabbasi et al. 2021; Casino-García et al. 2019; Ogurlu 2021). High-ability students are more adaptable but less able to manage stress or to control their impulsivity and sometimes underestimate their emotional competence.

Subjective wellbeing

Subjective wellbeing (SWB) is how students define and evaluate themselves as a result of their social interactions. This includes their feelings of social connection versus vulnerability and the level of anxiety or stress they feel during social interactions. SWB has 3 elements: the student's judgements of life satisfaction, their level of positive emotion or affect and their level of negative emotion. It is determined by the balance between their positive and negative emotion. While high-ability and gifted students generally have higher positive self-concepts, some have experiences with their teachers and peers that lead to negative feelings and behaviours (for example, boredom, loneliness, anxiety, confusion, rejection, bullying and victimisation). Some are aware of their asynchronous development in the social and emotional areas. Factors such as the type of high-ability and gifted learning profile, educational adjustment, EI and personality influence SWB.

Intuitively, high ability and giftedness could have either a positive or a negative effect on SWB. It equips individuals to understand others and their world better and to adapt socially; for example, to deal better with conflicts. However, it can also lead to social vulnerability and increased experience of the negative moods noted earlier. This is more likely in classrooms in which the culture and climate are not differentiated to support high-ability and gifted students' learning activity.

High-ability and gifted students did not differ from their regular-learning peers in judging satisfaction with life generally. However, their school experiences influenced their overall life satisfaction more than for their regular peers. Perfectionism is linked with different components of SWB; positive or functional perfectionism is linked with satisfaction with life and positive affect, while negative perfectionism is linked with negative mood.

For students who have begun to form an EI, you might expect the 3 categories of social–emotional capacities to be linked as shown in Figure 11.2.

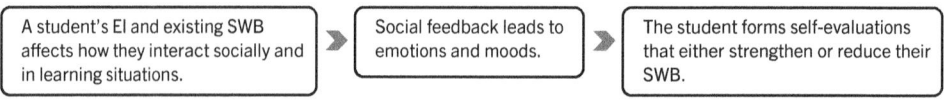

Figure 11.2. Links between students' emotional intelligence (EI) and subjective wellbeing (SWB)

Teacher and peer support are linked positively with students' wellbeing. Classroom tasks and challenges that match a high-ability and gifted profile are more likely to lead to positive emotions than challenges that either are too easy or too difficult. When the student is intrinsically motivated, can exercise self-agency and interact positively with peers, wellbeing is more likely to be positive.

Explaining social–emotional issues in terms of high-ability and gifted learning

We can explain the emotional or social problems of high-ability and gifted students partly in terms of the intuitive theories they form about possible personal events in their lives.

High-ability students don't restrict their ability to infer, evaluate and synthesise to academic learning. Chapter 5 noted that they can infer about their experiences, including their social interactions. They generate possibilities and intuitive theories about events that might happen. They may judge that they don't have either the social or experiential skill for responding to the theories they form. They may perceive themselves as not coping or failing, feel threatened and display negative emotional behaviours; for example, self-doubt.

This is shown in the sequence presented in Figure 11.3.

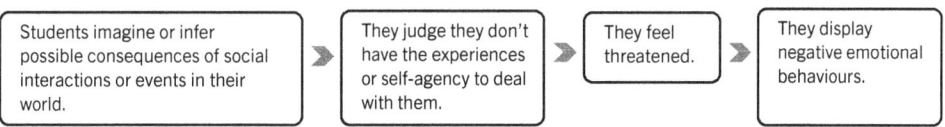

Figure 11.3. How students' inferences can affect social–emotional wellbeing

Schools can help these students manage their negative emotional reactions by guiding them to deal more functionally with their negative intuitive theories. This involves scaffolding them to improve their EI. Procedures for doing this are outlined in the next section.

High-ability and gifted students are generally as socially and emotionally competent as their peers (Cross et al. 2008). Issues that arise can often be linked with their advanced learning capacity and their environmental interactions. Some of these students display difficulties such as depression, anxiety and isolation. Some are more sensitive to the social needs of their regular peers than the reverse. Educational opportunities that match their high-ability and gifted profile can often lower their social-emotional needs and challenges.

Strategies to support high-ability and gifted students with social-emotional challenges

High-ability students who have social-emotional challenges in managing their moods, their EI or SWB may need support in and beyond the classroom. Many will need external professional psychological counselling and guidance. Any work done in the classroom needs to be aligned with, and informed by, external support.

In the classroom, teachers can unpack a student's social-emotional competence. The Collaborative for Academic, Social, and Emotional Learning (CASEL) (Oberle et al. 2016) provides one option in its identification of 5 social-emotional competencies. The teaching framework (see CASEL 2023) is described in detail here so that leaders know what it 'looks like' and can plan how to implement it within the school's structure. A high-ability and gifted student with social-emotional issues may need assistance in some of these areas of competence.

Self-awareness

Some students need help to understand and accept their emotions, thoughts and values and how they influence behaviour across contexts. Teaching can help them to:

> ❯ understand and accept who they are
> ❯ identify their emotions, positive and negative, and how they are elicited

> deal with asynchronous development issues that can restrict their progress

> understand their self-efficacy in various contexts and its impact on their thinking and learning

> deal with their 'mental energy'.

Self-management

Some students have difficulty managing and regulating their emotions and behaviours in various contexts to achieve their goals and intentions. They need scaffolding to:

> become aware of how and what they tell themselves about situations (their self-talk), its link with their emotional responses, how they can see alternative ways of talking about situations and how this can enhance their social–emotional competence

> use coping strategies to manage and regulate intense emotional responses, such as high anxiety, stress, depression and heightened sensitivities

> use personal agency; for example, how to plan a path through difficult situations or how to take risks

> manage their expectations of themselves and others; deal with negative perfectionism

> deal with vulnerability related to creativity

> learn how to set and pursue goals.

Social awareness

Some students have difficulty understanding and empathising with the perspectives of others, including those from other backgrounds. They can be assisted to:

- ❯ 'read' social situations and infer how others feel or think (that is, improve their theory of mind), show concern or empathy for others, show gratitude
- ❯ use how other high-ability and gifted individuals manage their lives as options and models for themselves
- ❯ identify other individuals' capacities and strengths
- ❯ identify social norms and deal with social justice and world issues that worry them
- ❯ understand how cultures and institutions influence how individuals act and make decisions
- ❯ deal with negative school experiences.

Relationship skills

Some students have difficulty developing and maintaining healthy and supportive relationships. Teaching can help them to:

- ❯ improve their social peer group interaction skills, manage loneliness and social isolation
- ❯ learn positive, useful attitudes to others
- ❯ interact and communicate effectively and in culturally appropriate ways
- ❯ work collaboratively to solve problems and achieve team goals, both as a member and a leader
- ❯ constructively negotiate interpersonal issues such as conflicts
- ❯ provide support when appropriate
- ❯ defend the rights of others; resist negative social pressure.

Responsible decision-making

Some students have difficulty planning and regulating their personal and social interaction behaviour across situations. Teaching can guide them to:

- think analytically and evaluatively and make ethical judgements for personal and social wellbeing
- infer possible solutions for personal and social challenges
- anticipate and evaluate the consequences of their actions
- plan how to act to foster personal, family and community wellbeing.

The support teachers provide in these areas will probably be informal, relevant to particular contexts and advisory; suggesting possible options, rather than formal intervention. The intensity and breadth of a student's issues at any time will determine the complexity of the assistance needed. Health and wellbeing professionals can recommend to teachers the specific aspects to target and how best to do this in the classroom. The informal support can include:

- providing opportunities for students to practise and apply what they learn in the professional counselling
- providing corrective feedback
- building self-efficacy and positive self-identity
- modelling how to use self-talk and planning in personal and social situations, and how students can identify the options they have.

What your school can do now

Social and emotional issues can restrict the learning progress of all students, including the high-ability and gifted students. Provision for these students in your school will be improved when your staff is better equipped to recognise these issues and to respond to them within the course of regular educational practice.

Connect with health and wellbeing professionals

Establish links with health and wellbeing professionals who have expertise in social-emotional issues and who can support high-ability and gifted students who have these issues. The school can provide opportunities for individual staff to consult with these professionals in relation to unpacking individual students' social-emotional issues and supporting the students in the classroom.

Enhance staff awareness

Enhance staff awareness of social-emotional issues by unpacking and evaluating the content in this chapter. Regular teaching frequently assumes students have a range of social and emotional capacities. Some students display inappropriate or negative social and/or emotional behaviours in the classroom that fluctuate in their intensity and/or frequency. These can be perplexing, challenging, difficult to handle and somewhat random. They can mask the student's high-ability and gifted learning profile and can restrict their achievement.

Provide workshops led by health and wellbeing professionals

Workshops led by the health and wellbeing professionals can unpack the characteristics of high-ability and gifted students who have social-emotional issues. This can focus on understanding how these students learn and on separating the social-emotional capacities from other aspects of the high-ability and gifted learning profile.

These workshops can examine procedures for identifying social-emotional issues in the classroom. Social-emotional issues can be linked with the learning demands and the classroom climate and culture. Classroom teachers are usually not trained to diagnose these types of issues. They can observe displays of inappropriate or negative social and/or emotional behaviours in the classroom that fluctuate in their intensity and/or frequency. These can include withdrawal and disengagement, stress and anxiety, anger and aggression, depression or feelings of persecution. Tools such as the Overexcitability Questionnaire

(Falk et al. 1999) described in Chapter 7 can assist in identifying and interpreting these behaviours. Staff can describe, share and unpack inappropriate social and emotional problems they have observed high-ability and gifted students display and the contexts in which they occurred. From these observations, they can compile a checklist that teachers can use to identify these issues in the future.

Training facilitated by health and wellbeing professionals can recommend strategies to support students, in the classroom and in informal individual counselling sessions in which teachers offer practical guidance. The teacher here is not operating as a health and wellbeing expert but is instead supporting the student to optimise their achievements. Practical guidance includes fostering a safe and supportive classroom and peer group culture, differentiating the teaching and helping students see options for dealing with issues. Some students, on occasion, may feel overwhelmed with negative emotion. The teacher can discuss actions they can take to deal with this in supporting, accepting ways. This can help students improve their ability to manage their emotions

The health and wellbeing professionals can also recommend ways of monitoring, reviewing and modifying the support and guidance procedures used. They can suggest the indicative behavioural data teachers can collect about individual students. This can include the extent to which the student displays overall wellbeing, positive self-efficacy, a preparedness to engage with the teaching, the student's ability to effectively manage an increasing range of social–emotional demands and being more able to display their learning profile consistently and achieve high-level outcomes. Inviting comment and feedback from students and tapping into the student voice is a key aspect of this data collection.

Summary

The link between high learning ability and social–emotional issues is complex. It can impact on students' overall wellbeing and world views and on their success in achieving their potential.

Three characteristics are relevant: a student's emotional state or mood, their ability to perceive, understand, manage and use emotions (their emotional intelligence), and how they 'know themselves' through social interactions. The relationship between these characteristics and high ability is 'bi-directional'; the characteristics affect learning and vice versa.

The emotional or social problems high-ability and gifted students display can be explained partly in terms of the intuitive theories they form about events in their lives. They infer possible events from their experiences that they believe they cannot control. They feel threatened, alone and alienated, which leads to self-doubt.

High-ability students who have social–emotional challenges can be assisted in the classroom by differentiated teaching that targets self-awareness and acceptance of emotions, learning to manage and regulate their emotions, learning to understand and empathise with the perspectives of others and developing and maintaining healthy and supportive relationships. The support teachers provide in these areas is more likely to be informal and advisory and involve suggesting possible options. Health and wellbeing professionals can recommend to teachers the specific aspects to target and how best to do this in the classroom.

References

Abdulla Alabbasi AM, A. Ayoub AE and Ziegler A (2021) 'Are gifted students more emotionally intelligent than their non-gifted peers? A meta-analysis', *High Ability Studies*, 32(2):189–217, doi:10.1080/13598139.2020.1770704.

CASEL (Collaborative for Academic, Social, and Emotional Learning) (2023) *SEL in the classroom*, CASEL website, CASEL, Chicago, IL, accessed 2 November 2023. https://casel.org/systemic-implementation/sel-in-the-classroom/

Casino-García AM, García-Pérez J and Llinares-Insa LI (2019) 'Subjective emotional well-being, emotional intelligence, and mood of gifted vs. unidentified students: a relationship model', *International journal of Environmental Research and Public Health*, 16(18):3266, doi:10.3390/ijerph16183266.

Colangelo N and Wood SM (2015) 'Counseling the gifted: past, present, and future directions', *Journal of Counseling & Development*, 93(2):133–142.

Cross TL, Cassady JC, Dixon, FA and Adams CM (2008) 'The psychology of gifted adolescents as measured by the MMPI-A', *Gifted Child Quarterly*, 52(4):326–339, doi:10.1177/0016986208321810.

Falk RF, Lind S, Miller NB, Piechowski MM and Silverman LK (1999) *The Overexcitabilities Questionnaire-Two (OEQII)*, Institute for the Study of Advanced Development, Denver, CO.

Foley Nicpon M, Doobay AF and Assouline SG (2010) 'Parent, teacher, and self-perceptions of psychosocial functioning in intellectually gifted children and adolescents with autism spectrum disorder', *Journal of Autism and Developmental Disorders*, 40:1028–1038, doi:10.1007/s10803-010-0952-8.

Oberle E, Domitrovich CE, Meyers DC and Weissberg RP (2016) 'Establishing systemic social and emotional learning approaches in schools: a framework for schoolwide implementation', *Cambridge Journal of Education*, 46(3):277–297, doi:10.1080/0305764X.2015.1125450.

Ogurlu U (2021) 'A meta-analytic review of emotional intelligence in gifted individuals: a multilevel analysis', *Personality and Individual Differences*, 171:110503, doi:10.1016/j.paid.2020.110503.

CHAPTER 12

Learning from high-ability and gifted students

Introduction

So far, the focus has been on what educators and researchers say about high-ability and gifted provision. Teachers and students sometimes differ in what they think comprises effective provision (Chandra Handa 2020). In this chapter, the focus is on what the students, key stakeholders in this provision, can tell us.

Chapter 4 noted how high-ability and gifted students usually develop an awareness of how and when they learn most successfully. Their enhanced metacognitive skill equips them to have thoughtful, reflective understanding of how they learn, the teaching and climate conditions that work for them and ideas for how the provision can be improved.

The students' perspectives can provide school leaders with insights into high-ability and gifted educational provision. They can tell the leadership:

> how they prefer to learn and to be taught

> how they perceive current provision in the school and the extent to which the curriculum, teaching, classroom culture and climate helps them learn

> how they believe provision could be improved; what their 'ideal' provision would look like.

The focus of this chapter is on how these students can be given the opportunity to share their perceptions and beliefs about how they know and learn and the conditions under which they can do this. The main ideas in this chapter are shown in Figure 12.1.

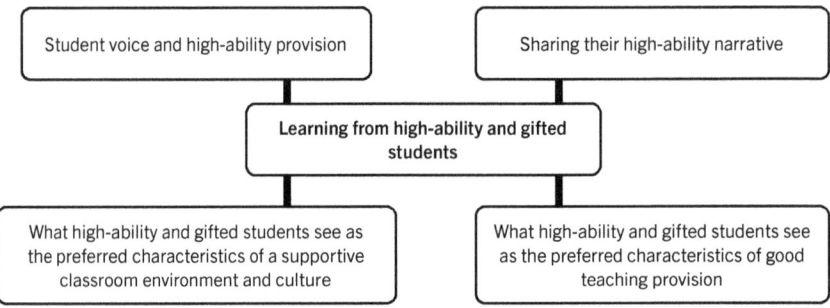

Figure 12.1. Learning from high-ability and gifted students

The student voice and high-ability and gifted provision

Student voice refers to students having the opportunity to influence school practices and educational provision (Mitra and Gross 2009). Students have unique knowledge and perspectives about these that can enhance future provision. High-ability students can participate in decision-making by sharing their experiences and reflections with educators in 3 ways. They can be invited to:

> share their school experiences; for example, by identifying practices and policies that either support or restrict their capacity to achieve talented outcomes, or aspects of the

school environment that impact on their social and academic wellbeing; educators can listen actively and discuss with the student their intended message and the implications for practice

> collaborate with educators to recommend how aspects of provision might be modified, sharing their perspectives on problems and possible solutions, such as how to improve curriculum differentiation, how student outcomes are assessed, teaching practice and teacher–student interactions. Some students may need time to reflect on specific challenges and problems and possible solutions

> take a broader leadership role in decisions about aspects of provision and be afforded the opportunity to analyse and evaluate school processes and structures; students may recommend additional curriculum options, alternative assessment protocols or a broader range of teaching practices.

Obviously, for the student voice to be effective, schools need to be prepared to listen actively and to have the structures and mechanisms that allow student voice to inform an innovation. Mitra and Gross (2009) note that when these structures are not well implemented, the student voice can lead to negative outcomes. These are less likely when the students are equipped to share their voice and understand and accept the intended purposes of collaborating. Some teachers may also feel threatened when participating with students in this way.

An issue for the school leadership is how to embed the opportunity for the student voice of high-ability and gifted students in the whole-school context. Some schools will already provide this opportunity for all students. Others that elect to do this only for high-ability and gifted students may need to plan ways to do this that avoid the criticism of preferencing this group.

Sharing their high-ability and gifted narrative

High-ability and gifted students learn differently from their regular peers. To achieve high-level outcomes, they need supportive environments. Schools can invite these students to describe and share:

> how they prefer to learn

> the approaches to teaching provision that work best for them

> the environmental aspects of classrooms that help them achieve high-level outcomes.

Schools can use a range of activities to invite students to explore and share how they prefer to learn and to be taught, such as those in which they compose and share their autobiography or story of their learning history or activities where they respond to interviews and surveys about their learning history. High-ability and gifted students are better equipped to share their voice when they have the opportunity to compose what they would like to share and to align it with the intended purposes of the sharing. They can reflect on, analyse and evaluate their learning history and synthesise a narrative of how they prefer to learn. They can use various open-ended questions to help them to prepare this, such as:

> In what areas have you achieved high-level outcomes and what did you do to learn them? How do you prefer to learn?

> What factors do you think affected your learning success?

> What teaching strategies helped you to learn well? What teaching restricted your learning?

> What would your ideal school and classroom look like? How would you like to see your current classroom and school change?

The students can write their autobiography, record it as an oral presentation in a video or prepare a multimodal presentation. The presentations can include photographs or videos of past achievements and descriptions of the thinking they used to achieve them. The opportunity to compose their learning autobiography equips the students to 'be heard'.

Teaching characteristics preferred by high-ability and gifted students

High-ability and gifted students can share their perspectives on teaching provision in a range of formats, including:

> - providing open-ended responses to a stimulus, such as 'What do you think a good teacher does?' Bakx et al. (2017) used a spider-map with primary school students. Rogers (2019) invited secondary students to describe the characteristics of their most and least effective teachers

> - through surveys that invite students to respond to descriptions of teacher behaviours in particular ways. Chandra Handa (2020) and Rogers (2019) used surveys with secondary students.

Research studies (Bakx et al. 2017; Chandra Handa 2020; Rogers 2019) differ in how they organise and analyse student contributions. Across the differences, it is possible to identify what high-ability and gifted students generally see as effective provision. Students in these studies valued:

> - teaching that was differentiated to match their individual learning profile. It displayed high expectations, provided challenge, linked with their interests and encouraged them to think flexibly for themselves; for example, divergently or evaluatively. It gave them the opportunity to make decisions, use their initiative and choose the direction for their learning and feel respected. They preferred their

teachers to have an expert knowledge of the subject and to understand what it means to teach high-ability and gifted students

> teaching support and structure, when appropriate. Their preference for the opportunity to learn autonomously was balanced with a desire for more teaching support and structure. They valued teaching that was well-organised, clear, covered the required content, defined unfamiliar concepts, explained ideas clearly and in everyday language, encouraged student comments and questions and allowed the students to show all that they knew

> positive, mutually accepting, trusting and respectful relationships with their teachers. They preferred teachers who were non-judgemental and open-minded, who valued individual differences and who related positively and showed personal interest

> safe, non-threatening learning environments that were learner-centred, respected students' interpretations, praised ideas and effort and made learning interesting.

In a case study of 900+ selective school students, Rogers (2019) notes that high-ability boys and girls at the secondary level differed in their perceptions of effective provision; girls more frequently valued teaching that understood and matched their learning profiles and that provided emotional support. Boys valued more the teacher's personality and relationship with them. The girls generally had lower self-esteem. The age of the secondary students also influenced the educational characteristics they preferred (Rogers 2019). Younger students valued more the quality of the teacher–student relationships and the extent to which the teachers understood and matched high-ability and gifted learning profiles in their teaching, whereas older students were more interested in the quality of the teaching.

These studies have important messages for school leaders. Their findings suggest that teachers:

- can improve how well they recognise, understand and use high-ability and gifted students' learning profiles
- should not assume that high-ability and gifted students will 'make it on their own', but instead be prepared to provide them with as much structure as other students
- should communicate high expectations to these students and present them with intellectually appropriate challenges.

Classroom climate and culture preferred by high-ability and gifted students

The critical role of the classroom climate and culture on the emergence of high-level and talented outcomes has been discussed in earlier chapters. This area has also been elaborated in research by Ziegler et al. (2017).

Teachers can invite students to share their perceptions of how the classroom culture has supported their high-ability and gifted learning in a range of ways:

- how it has provided the opportunity for them to learn optimally
- how teachers and peers have responded to their learning activity
- the level of infrastructure and material support provided.

Schools can initiate student contribution in these areas through open-ended discussion and the use of questionnaires.

The knowledge a school leadership can gain from listening to the student voice about the cultural and environmental support for high-ability and gifted provision can contribute to optimising provision.

What your school can do now

How ready is your school to listen to its high-ability and gifted students and to include them in the improvement activity? Some educators may be reluctant to engage with students in this process. They may need to learn more about it and the extent to which it can enhance the implementation. A discussion of Mitra and Gross' (2009) article and its relevance to improving provision could assist here.

The activities discussed here can be implemented when you judge your school is ready for its student voice and when your high-ability and gifted students are ready to engage with providing it. Schools can invite student contributions in these areas through presentations, open-ended individual and small group discussions and the use of questionnaires. The prompts for the discussions and items that could be included in the questionnaires are described in this chapter.

Discuss and review studies

The leadership team can lead discussion and review of the findings of the studies that report the voices of high-ability and gifted students (Bakx et al. 2017; Chandra Handa 2020; Rogers 2019) and the implications for their improved teaching provision. Teachers can reflect on what the findings would 'look like' in their practice and how to respond to the students' learning and teaching preferences.

Invite high-ability and gifted students to tell their story

Your leadership can plan activities in which the high-ability and gifted students compose their autobiographies that describe how they prefer to learn and to be taught. You can use the open-ended questions mentioned in this chapter to help them prepare. The leadership and teachers can plan how they will listen actively to each student's presentation and discuss and infer implications from it for practice.

Invite high-ability and gifted students to comment on the teaching

You can ask your high-ability and gifted students questions of the form, 'What does effective teaching for you look like?' You can use either the open-ended or survey formats to do this. To assist students in their responses or as part of the design of questionnaires or surveys, you can prompt students to comment on:

> ❯ their overall engagement with their class and school and their feelings about these
> ❯ their perceptions of how well the teaching supports their profiles, the learning opportunities they prefer and the extent to which teachers understand their learning profiles
> ❯ the relationships they prefer with teachers and the teacher personalities they value
> ❯ the teaching behaviours that work best for them
> ❯ their perceptions of the extent to which the classroom climate supports their profiles
> ❯ the infrastructure necessary to support their learning activity; this includes access to appropriate information sources, facilities and materials, environmental supports and the physical spaces that support high-ability and gifted learning and education.

Invite high-ability and gifted students to comment on classroom climate and culture

Students can be invited to share their perceptions of how the classroom culture has supported their high-ability and gifted learning and how it can be improved. Students can be asked:

> ❯ In what ways does classroom culture provide the opportunity for optimal learning? How could it be improved?
> ❯ How do teachers and peers respond to their high-ability learning activity?
> ❯ How sufficient are the infrastructure and materials provided to support learning?

Evaluate and interpret student information

Staff can collaboratively evaluate and interpret student information and:

> note what students identified as being in place and the modifications they would recommend

> unpack how the recommended modifications seen as appropriate could be implemented and discuss their possibilities with the high-ability and gifted students

> negotiate a modified approach to teaching and a way forward with these students.

Summary

High-ability students have unique knowledge and perspectives about what works in educational provision. This can enhance provision in the school.

This knowledge can be collected by inviting students to:

> share their experiences with educators

> respond to problems and issues in provision

> recommend ways of broadening the provision.

As a first step, schools can invite these students to describe and share their story of educational provision in the school. Students can include reference to how they prefer to learn, the approaches to teaching provision that worked best for them, how the environmental aspects of classrooms affected the achievement of high-level outcomes and how they would recommend modifying or differentiating the provision.

The student voice can be collected in a range of ways:

> open-ended formats that share the student narratives

> surveys that ask about their learning history.

Students are better equipped to share their voice when they have the opportunity to compose what they would like to share and to align it with the intended purposes of the sharing.

Research reports that high-ability and gifted students prefer teaching that:

> uses their learning profiles and shows a genuine interest in them

> does not assume that the students will 'make it on their own' (teaching that is still structured)

> communicates high expectations and presents them with intellectually appropriate challenges

> covers and communicates the content effectively

> is flexible, accepting, open-minded and encourages students to think for themselves

> fosters positive teacher–student relationships.

References

Bakx A, Van Houtert T, Brand MVD and Hornstra L (2017) 'A comparison of high-ability pupils' views vs. regular ability pupils' views of characteristics of good primary school teachers', *Educational Studies*, 45(1):35–56, doi:10.1080/03055698.2017.1390443.

Chandra Handa M (2020) 'Examining students' and teachers' perceptions of differentiated practices, student engagement, and teacher qualities', *Journal of Advanced Academics*, 31(4):530-568, doi:10.1177/1932202X20931457.

Mitra DL and Gross SJ (2009) 'Increasing student voice in high school reform: building partnerships, improving outcomes', *Educational Management Administration & Leadership*, 37(4):522–543, doi:10.1177/1741143209334577.

Rogers KB (2019) 'Australian teachers who made a difference: secondary gifted student perceptions of teaching and teacher effectiveness', in Smith SR (ed) *Handbook of giftedness and talent development in the Asia-Pacific,* Springer Nature Singapore Pty Ltd., Gateway East, Singapore.

Ziegler A and Stoeger H (2017) 'Systemic gifted education: a theoretical introduction', *Gifted Child Quarterly*, 61(3):183–193, doi:10.1177/0016986217705713.

CHAPTER 13

Implementing improved provision for high-ability and gifted students: a whole-school approach

Introduction

The 'What your school can do now' sections in earlier chapters focused on building the professional knowledge needed to support improved provision and recommending actions leaders can take to implement aspects of provision. We are now at the point of putting this professional knowledge into practice in a consistent, systematic whole-school way.

This is a 'What your school can do now' chapter. It examines how the leadership can synthesise the professional knowledge into an implementation strategy that is underpinned by the 'code of teaching practice' for high-ability and gifted provision mentioned in Chapter 1 (see p. 13). This practice is intended to achieve the school's goals of enhanced provision for these students.

The main ideas in this chapter are shown in Figure 13.1.

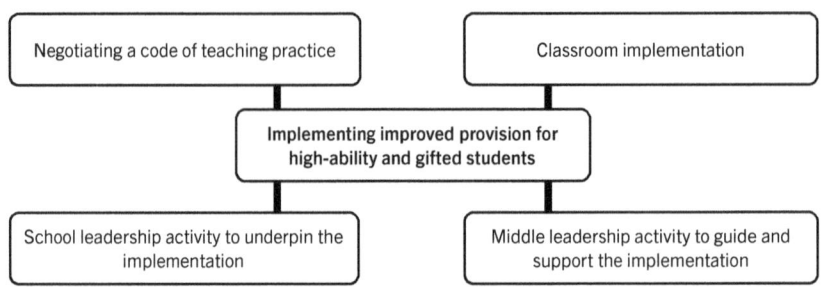

Figure 13.1. Implementing a whole-school strategy

Negotiating a code of teaching practice

The code of teaching practice for high-ability and gifted provision describes the differentiated pedagogy, curriculum and culture needed for effective provision. At the classroom level, it describes what modified provision for high-ability and gifted students would 'look like'. At the school-wide level, it specifies the teaching, curriculum differentiation and climate modification that will underpin the implementation of high-ability and gifted provision and describes how the school will achieve this vision and policy.

The code is compiled and developed though staff dialogue, reflection, and negotiation, led by the leadership or middle-level coaches. When leaders have guided staff through the content in Chapters 2 to 12, the leadership can take steps to draw together or synthesise what staff know now about high-ability provision. A code of teaching practice can be negotiated via the following process:

1. Staff discuss what they know now about high-ability and gifted learning and negotiate a shared perspective.
2. Staff infer and negotiate what modified provision for high-ability and gifted students would 'look like'.

Middle leaders or coaches of high-ability and gifted provision can lead staff to collate what they now know and believe about, and negotiate a shared understanding of, the following aspects:

> what high-ability and gifted learning and high-level outcomes and talent 'look like' in classrooms, the multiple high-ability and gifted learning profiles and the learning profiles of underachieving and twice-exceptional students

> how contextual and classroom culture and climate factors influence the conversion of high-ability and gifted understanding to high-level or talented outcomes

> how the multiple forms of high-ability learning profiles can be identified, through formal assessments and through students' interaction with teaching

> the emotional and social aspects of high-ability learning profiles and how these can be managed to optimise high-level outcomes

> how to differentiate the curriculum, teaching and classroom climate for high-ability students

> the roles and responsibilities of educators for high-ability students.

This collation provides an explicit and direct first step to improved provision for high-ability and gifted students. It provides teachers with a negotiated, shared framework for implementing provision and a common language for talking about it. Teachers can use it to guide and modify their practice for high-ability students. It helps teachers see the decisions they can make and the actions they can take to cater for these students. Also, knowing that teachers share a common approach with their colleagues that is available for modification based on their in-practice evaluation can increase their preparedness to engage.

A collation of knowledge also allows the leadership to identify a school-wide professional knowledge base that can underpin and guide future provision. It can inform school-level policies, structures and processes to support high-ability and gifted students; for example, through processes for early entry, year-level acceleration, involvement with external educational institutions and agencies and fostering talent development at a school level.

It is important to the success of the implementation that potential differences and inconsistencies in participants' understanding of key issues to do with the provision are negotiated and possibly resolved through dialogue at this point. Chandra Handa (2019), for example, reported a difference between teachers and leaders in a school in their perceptions of the extent to which differentiated teaching strategies were being implemented. It is recommended that leaders allocate time to developing a shared perspective and language for high-ability provision.

Schools differ in how they approach implementation. For this reason, this chapter does not recommend a single code of teaching practice. Instead, it describes a range of activities leadership teams can use. They can select the activities most relevant to their context at any time.

The implementation strategy

The code of teaching practice for high ability and giftedness describes what the changed provision looks like. The whole-school implementation strategy describes how to implement it. This requires parallel and aligned activity at 3 levels or roles in the school:

1. Implementation of modified provision in the classroom. This is the modified curriculum, teaching procedures and climate that will be implemented systematically and gradually.

2. School-wide leadership activities that provide infrastructure and support for the classroom implementation and coordinate the provision at the whole-school level.

3. Middle-level leadership activity that guides the classroom implementation and informs the work of the leadership team. The middle leaders coordinate, guide and monitor the activity in individual classrooms and advise the leadership

of the progress and necessary adjustments. This role is unpacked in a later section.

Classroom implementation

The school's vision and goals for improved provision need to be interpreted as goals in each classroom for high-ability students and for their teachers. Each teacher needs a classroom implementation plan for the gradual differentiation of teaching. Each plan specifies how progress towards the goals will be monitored.

Chapters 8 to 10 noted how regular provision in classrooms can be modified in a range of ways. These included the various versions of acceleration and content-based approaches to differentiation. The focus here is on content-based approaches to implementation for high-ability students in classrooms with same-age regular learning peers. It also has relevance to the various types of acceleration; high-ability and gifted students continue to use their gifted learning profiles in these contexts, even though the curriculum is more advanced.

Each teacher's implementation activity needs to be informed by continuing access to professional learning. This includes the opportunity to work collaboratively and to share their emerging knowledge and experience with colleagues.

It is likely that successful classroom implementation will require teachers to engage in the activities discussed here.

Teachers interpret available data for learning profiles

The data for the learning profiles of high-ability and gifted students may include formal assessments of a student's learning profile, earlier achievement data and in-situ classroom learning information. It can include past and present information and can also include current 'student voice' data described in Chapter 12.

The goal of the interpretation is to identify individual students' knowledge, learning and thinking strengths and challenges, how they engage with classroom teaching, how they see themselves as a learner (including self-identity, self-efficacy, interests and patterns in their intrinsic motivation) and how they perceive their social interaction skills. These procedures are described throughout Chapter 7.

Teachers set modified outcome goals

Goal setting provides a direction for the differentiated provision and valuing of high-ability and gifted students. There are 2 types of outcome goals that teachers can plan:

> Broad-based goals that take account of the student's learning profile:

- These refer generally to the quality of understanding a student might form; for example, a high-ability student will form an understanding that is more sophisticated than their peers, with several additional inferred concepts that are organised hierarchically with meaningful relationships and possibilities.

> Specific goals that refer to particular topics being taught:

- Teachers can generate the specific goals by embedding the broad-based goals in topics or domains they will teach. Chapter 8 describes how to differentiate the curriculum to identify higher levels of knowledge and understanding that these students can be taught. These higher levels can be used to generate the specific goals for a student.

Teachers plan summative assessment of high-level outcomes

Linked with setting the curriculum goals for high-ability students are the summative assessment tasks that teachers will use to assess acquisition of the goals by individual students. For any topic, teachers can plan the tasks they will use to assess various high-level and talented outcomes. These procedures are described in Chapters 2 and 6 (see p. 17 and p. 73).

Teachers differentiate regular provision

One of the ways regular provision can be differentiated is through teachers planning a differentiated curriculum and units of student work. They can collaborate, sharing their areas of expertise or interest to enrich the units and can be guided in these activities by middle leaders.

Teachers can differentiate any topic by modifying the curriculum, teaching and climate for the multiple high-ability learning profiles, twice-exceptional students and high-ability students from diverse cultural backgrounds. The procedures associated with this are described in Chapters 7 to 10.

Classroom implementation through differentiation also involves decisions about the classroom climate and culture, student groupings and timing considerations. These include planning for involvement in acceleration or withdrawal programs and facilitating working with mentors and working in small group activities in the classroom. Classroom teachers also need to manage and monitor the range of resources they need to support high-ability provision.

A classroom implementation plan needs to give teachers the opportunity to explore and evaluate differentiating particular components of their provision at any time. It needs to allow teachers to learn how to implement the components gradually in 'digestible' steps, possibly over several months.

Teachers use formative assessment to monitor student learning

Chapters 3 and 4 noted that high-ability and gifted students differ from their regular learning peers in their interpretations of teaching information and in their responses to classroom challenges. For effective provision, teachers need to identify instances of high levels of interpretation in students' responses and outcomes as they interact with the teaching. They need to evaluate what the students know at the time and use this to modify or differentiate their teaching by making both 'in the moment' and more long-term decisions.

Teachers can also monitor how high-ability students respond in the plethora of other interactions in the classroom. This includes how they interact socially and collaboratively with peers and how they manage their learning activity independently and take responsibility for this. Teachers can also track the progress of these students when aspects of the teaching or the classroom climate are modified.

Teachers are more able to make these formative assessment judgements when they have a sufficiently well-developed understanding of how these students learn and can apply this practically in the classroom. Without this knowledge, they are less able to observe and interpret students' behaviours and 'see' patterns in them. Classroom implementation needs to help teachers acquire these interpretative skills.

Teachers monitor the efficacy of the differentiated provision

Implementation in individual classrooms will be more successful if teachers can regularly monitor how well it is working and fine-tune it where necessary. Strategic monitoring of differentiation implementation is a type of formative assessment for the teacher; providing pointers as to how the differentiation can be improved. A plan for progressively monitoring the implementation's success can help teachers to fine tune and modify it if necessary.

Teachers can do this more effectively if they specify what they will use as indicators of success of the implementation. These include student learning indicators and teacher indicators. The latter include changes in teacher practice, professional knowledge about providing for high-ability students and teachers' self-efficacy, confidence and motivation to do this.

The implementation can also have unanticipated outcomes that can inform evaluation of its success. An example is when high-ability students who, prior to an intervention were disengaged from classroom activities, now become more engaged and share their high-level understanding. Teachers can see these changes in students' dispositions when they know what to look for.

The student voice is a valuable resource for informing ongoing monitoring of differentiation implementation. High-ability students can share their evaluation of the changed teaching at any time, how well it worked for them, how it could be modified or improved or how they would like the climate to be different.

This element of classroom implementation needs to be systematic and gradual and should be guided by an action plan. It also needs to be supported by a professional learning program that focuses on the classroom investigative and reflective activity by each teacher and the subsequent collaborative dialogue with colleagues. It can be led by middle leaders.

School-wide leadership activity

Classroom implementation needs to be supported by the school leadership. The 'What your school can do now' section of Chapter 1 describes a range of activities that provide a foundation for the leadership activities.

Use the vision and goals for enhanced provision to provide a focus leadership activity

The first activity in the 'What your school can do now' section of Chapter 1 refers to defining the school's vision and long-term general goal for the provision. The leadership team can use the vision and overarching goal to:

> unpack explicitly the reason, purpose or need for the change

> specify explicitly the subsequent goals for the school, for student outcomes and for teaching

> check that the goals are realistic for the school at that time and are aligned with the school community

> decide how progress towards the goals will be monitored and the indicators the school will use

> take steps to communicate the goals with the various stakeholders. Teachers, students, parents and carers and the broader community need to understand, accept, value and support the goals. Leadership needs to develop a unity of purpose regarding teaching goals and goal congruence among staff, encouraging staff to engage with these goals.

Develop the action plan

The action plan (the start of which was touched on in Chapter 1) needs to put the vision into practice, identify the expected roles and activities or participants, specify how progress will be monitored and specify the indicators of success that will be used. It also needs to be evaluated and refined as the implementation continues and new goals need to be negotiated. The plan should:

> be realistic and identify procedures for negotiating ownership by faculties and teachers

> take account of the composition of the regular classroom. Some regular learning students may find the novel differentiation practices challenging and possibly threatening. The plan needs to include strategies to orient all students to the differentiated provision and how they can learn best in this context. All students can respond to differentiated teaching, even though they differ in what they learn and how they do it.

Plan strategic actions for leading professional learning

This is critical for successful implementation. The strategic actions the leadership team can take are shown in Table 13.1. These need to be embedded in the specific context and culture of each school. The leadership can specify and plan how it will embed or 'do' each type of action in its context. The table is indicative of a template that your school's leadership team could use to record specific steps in relation to the strategic actions listed here. The key focus here is on strategic planning in these areas by the leadership team. Inadequate planning can restrict the success of the implementation.

Table 13.1. Strategic actions for the leadership team

STRATEGIC ACTIONS The leadership team can:	STEPS THE TEAM WILL TAKE
assess or estimate the professional knowledge and pedagogic strength required to achieve the goals.	
identify the current level of staff knowledge regarding the education of gifted and talented students.	
foster a school-wide professional learning culture to support the initiative; for example, to implement the recommendations about how to differentiate the teaching. Leadership can enhance staff awareness about high-ability learning and teaching by advocating for it in staff meetings, encouraging reflection and dialogue, planning for short-term successes and explicitly recognising teacher achievements and discoveries.	

guide teachers to implement aspects of the code of teaching practice for high-ability provision, and clarify expectations for these students, to work individually or in teams to trial and evaluate teaching procedures and pool what they learn professionally.	
foster the voice of high-ability students. This includes providing the opportunity for these students to be involved in contributing to the enhanced provision. It also includes communicating to them that they are valued for what they know and how they think and that they are encouraged to learn optimally and to share what they know.	
foster commitment to the school's agenda for improvement as a valued part of the school's overall direction and encourage staff to engage with it.	
plan how the enhanced high-ability provision will be staffed; for example, the roles of regular teachers, specialists, other professionals and mentors and how staff may be selected for the various roles.	
plan the space and time aspects of the enhanced high-ability provision; for example, where it will be implemented, the student groupings the school will use (e.g. regular classroom versus special classes or withdrawal), when it will be implemented (e.g. during the school week or out of school hours) and how long it will last.	
determine and manage the range of resources needed to support the improved provision. The provision will probably need economic, material and personnel support. This includes setting up and resourcing a group of middle leaders or coaches.	

Middle leadership activity

The middle leadership team can provide invaluable input and support to the work of the school leadership. Middle leaders are usually closer to and more in touch with what is happening in classrooms as an implementation progresses. They are aware of specific gains made and challenges that arise. They are well placed to recommend modifications and fine-tuning to the implementation.

Middle leadership activity works at the interface between leadership and classroom activity. It links them and leads and supports implementation in individual classrooms. Middle leaders operate as 'instructional team leaders' of high-ability and gifted provision. They foster dialogue about how to identify and to teach these students, they help build individual and team-level professional knowledge and provide supportive feedback to colleagues. Their work as a bridge between leadership activity and classroom activity is shown in Figure 13.2.

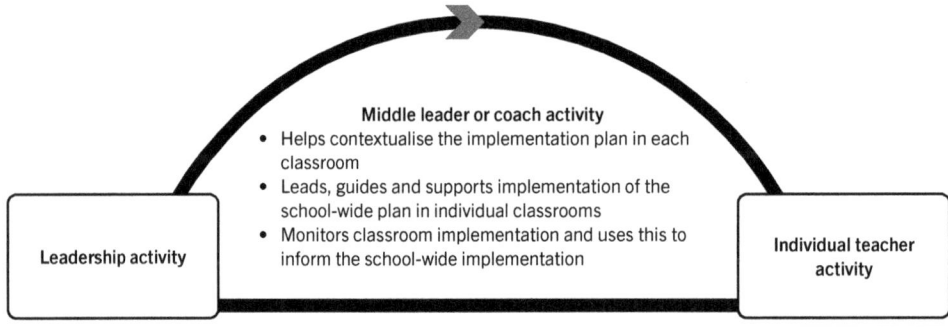

Figure 13.2. Middle leaders linking leadership and classroom activities

Much like metacognition guides learning activity in individual learners, the work of middle leaders, or coaches, guides group learning. Middle leaders will work with groups such as year levels, faculty or department teams and with individual teachers and offer a range of guidance and support.

Middle leadership guidance for teachers and groups of teachers

Middle leaders can guide staff to put the school's policy, including its code of practice, into practice in the form of explicit outcomes for their provision for high-ability and gifted students and to set goals for teachers and students. Teachers can be encouraged to visualise what classroom provision will 'look like' for them when the school-wide vision, goals and policy are realised. The middle leaders can guide teachers to unpack the implementation plan in their context and to identify what they already know and can do about putting it into action.

Some teachers may perceive barriers to the implementation. The middle leaders can guide teachers to respond to these by recommending ways around them, possibly by providing additional knowledge and alternative perspectives. These obstacles can frequently be reduced by analysing them from a teaching and learning perspective and identifying all that the teacher can do to resolve them.

Middle leaders guide teacher action plans

Middle leaders can guide teachers to develop action plans that build on students' learning profiles and that specify:

> - how differentiated practice will be gradually implemented in classrooms
> - indicators for monitoring improvement and growth in provision
> - procedures for data collection and for modification of provision.

The planning includes guiding teachers to interpret the available data that describes the learning profiles for individual high-ability and gifted students in their class and to identify its curriculum, teaching and climate implications. Teachers then map the data into learning outcomes and differentiated goals for these students.

The action plan for each teacher breaks the implementation into manageable or 'digestible' components that are 'do-able'. It will probably include plans for differentiating topics they will teach (see Chapter 8), and for their teaching by scaffolding high-ability and gifted thinking (see Chapter 9).

An action plan should also consider teaching materials and the classroom climate and structure. Middle leaders can guide teachers to select teaching materials and programs to support the differentiation for high-ability and gifted students to permit more rapid progress through the regular curriculum. Programs and stimulus materials can be assessed in terms of their appropriateness and practicality in the context, their breadth or comprehensiveness, their flexibility or adaptability and their validity (that is, how well they achieve their intended purposes with high-ability and gifted students).

The middle leader can also guide decisions relating to the classroom climate and arrangements. These include the grouping a teacher might use and for what purposes; for example, cross-age grouping, regrouping for specific instruction, cluster grouping, separate classes or cooperative learning.

Leading an 'in situ' professional development agenda

For successful implementation, some teachers may need to directly observe aspects of the high-ability and gifted provision being displayed in their classrooms. The middle leadership can practically demonstrate these aspects.

Some teachers may need guidance in recognising instances of high-ability and gifted learning in their teaching. Middle leaders can observe and monitor teaching sessions, identify instances of possible high-ability and gifted thinking and draw attention to these. The leaders can also recommend teaching procedures that are more likely to elicit evidence of high-ability and gifted learning.

Teachers may also need assistance with differentiating the curriculum. Middle leaders can guide teachers to apply the procedures described in Chapter 8 to topics they will teach. They can also recommend how to monitor the effectiveness of this differentiation for high-ability and gifted students.

Middle leaders can also model differentiated teaching procedures, which teachers can benefit from observing in their classrooms. The leaders can show how to integrate novel differentiated teaching procedures into regular teaching regimes and discuss with teachers how they might differentiate topics. Middle leaders can move towards the goal of ensuring that each topic is modified to cater for the learning profiles of gifted and talented students.

Middle leaders guide the implementation of a supportive classroom culture and climate

Chapter 10 describes the key indicators of a classroom culture and climate that fosters high-ability and gifted learning and the emergence of talented outcomes. Middle leaders can use these indicators to develop procedures such as observational checklists to assess and monitor the classroom climate in their school. They can use these checklists to evaluate current provision in classrooms and to guide teachers to identify how they might fine-tune or differentiate their culture and climate in the future.

The middle leaders can guide teachers to identify the extent to which the culture and climate in their classroom values more complex interpretations of the teaching, including those that are unique and unexpected. They can monitor how a teacher recognises and responds to displays of advanced, unusual student understanding and how the teacher uses this to enhance the understanding of all students in the class. They can use the checklists in collegiate 'shadowing' activities to record their observations of teacher activity and suggest, if appropriate, additional ways of overtly valuing high-level student outcomes.

The middle leaders can also review the range of opportunities the classroom culture provides for high-ability and gifted learning profiles to be displayed and for high-level learning behaviours to be valued. The classroom culture needs to value, foster and scaffold enquiry about one's world, curiosity and the open-ended pursuit of knowledge. It needs to foster students' self-agency as learners. This will be indicated in the dialogue about knowing and learning and the extent to which the culture encourages and values self-directed learning opportunities and problem-solving and the opportunity for students to inform procedures used to assess their outcomes. The culture also needs to allow students to show all they know about a topic in a range of ways, including their creative thinking about it.

The extent to which students are encouraged to evaluate and comment on how the classroom climate accommodates their learning profiles can also be examined. The culture needs to foster students' self-efficacy as learners. Middle leaders can examine the processes used to collect and interpret such data from high-ability and gifted students. Student voice data can indicate the extent of alignment of the classroom climate with how valued high-ability and gifted students feel and how safe, accepting and non-judgemental they find it. Students can comment on the opportunity they have for independent, self-directed and intrinsically motivated learning.

Middle leaders can guide teachers to monitor the extent to which they implement a flexible classroom organisation that provides the opportunity for various grouping options. These include access to collaborative learning with like-minded peers, to mentors (possibly through virtual interaction) and to learning centres with activities that vary in complexity and foster learning in multiple contexts. The leaders can also examine the range of resources available in the classroom to support individual investigation and interests. These include an appropriate range of information sources.

Many high-ability and gifted students benefit from a classroom culture that tolerates diverse social competence skills and that provides the opportunity to improve their social awareness and interaction skills and to learn acceptable social behaviours and conventions. These skills help high-ability and gifted students develop rapport with their peers and to share their advanced knowledge and understanding successfully. The middle leaders can observe and monitor the quality of social interactions in the classroom and the tolerance of difference and can assist teachers to modify this where necessary.

High-ability students frequently experience cognitive stress and anxiety. Some students, for example, display perfectionist traits. These are shown in the unrealistic demands and expectations they place on themselves and/or others. Negative emotions can arise in part because the students perceive the classroom context and culture to be threatening in particular ways. These emotions can significantly limit the student's ability to generate high-level outcomes and can be perplexing for classroom teachers. The middle leaders can assist teachers to recognise some of the characteristics of this stress; for example, a fear of failure, a propensity for self-criticism, a seeking of reassurance and unrealistic goal setting. They can also suggest ways in which the classroom climate and culture can be modified to lower the likelihood of these emotions in the future.

Collating emerging professional knowledge

Implementation is more likely to be successful when it is underpinned by an emerging explicit collaborative professional knowledge that is informed by teacher practice.

As staff explore and trial novel aspects of the provision in their teaching, they are likely to discover unexpected new ideas and useful teaching procedures and to design new learning activities and materials. These could potentially contribute to the professional knowledge of colleagues, enhance the learning of all students and extend the code of teaching practice. This can encourage teachers to take ownership of the innovation.

Middle leaders, in their role as the 'metacognition' of professional learning, can manage, guide and direct the collation of emerging professional knowledge and use it to support further learning. They can facilitate individual and group knowledge building by identifying the existing knowledge of staff at any time, scaffolding them to develop this by fostering dialogue about how to identify and teach high-ability and gifted students and by providing supportive feedback to colleagues. This knowledge can include growing a teaching and curriculum resource bank. It can also encourage staff to work collegiately.

The middle leaders can lead professional learning teams to trial teaching procedures in action research projects, identify the most effective teaching for use with high-ability and gifted students and add these to the team's code of teaching practice. An applied research focus encourages teachers to explore, speculate and generate possibilities that lead to further exploration and enhanced professional knowledge.

Middle leaders assist in monitoring the success of the provision

In addition to the action plan for each teacher mentioned on p. 223, middle leaders can work with staff to develop a set of indicators that monitor the success of the implementation. These indicators can be used to assess the efficacy of the modified pedagogy and inform future planning. Two types of indicators can be used: those that review and evaluate the modified teaching provision and those that monitor student engagement and the emergence of high-level outcomes. These indicators will show the extent to which teachers are moving towards their goals and the goals of the implementation more generally. They will also show whether it is necessary to take alternative activity.

It is expected that as the implementation proceeds, teachers will modify and differentiate the curriculum, their teaching and classroom culture in increasingly sophisticated ways. Middle leaders can assist teachers to monitor their progress in this activity and to plan and identify indicators they will use. Teachers can identify how their provision might be different and change each month. It is also expected that the engagement and outcomes of high-ability and gifted students will change as the implementation proceeds. Middle leaders can assist teachers to identify indicators of increased student engagement, enhanced learning opportunities and the emergence of high-level outcomes.

The 2 indicators are linked. Each teacher can be assisted to identify the formative assessment data they will use to track the progress of high-ability and gifted students. They can unpack how they will use the formative assessment procedures to make 'in the moment' teaching decisions about differentiation.

They can also identify the tasks they will use to assess the quality of student outcomes summatively. These procedures are described in Chapters 2 and 6. The monitoring may also lead to teachers negotiating new goals and directions in the topic or the subject.

Middle leaders and families and the broader community

Middle leaders can examine ways of guiding the active support of families and the broader community for the improved provision.

Parents and carers differ in their understanding of high ability and giftedness and its implications for children, and families. They may need guidance to understand their child's learning profile, how it differs from those of their peers and how to interpret assessment data. They may also need to know the optimal teaching conditions for their child and how these will be implemented. Parents and carers may also need to unpack their role in supporting and scaffolding their child to achieve optimal outcomes and may need advice about possible social or emotional issues.

Middle leaders can collaborate to foster broader community support for the improved provision. The steps they take and the activities they implement will depend on the context of the school.

The professional knowledge of middle leaders

Middle leaders or coaches need sufficient professional knowledge of high-ability and gifted provision and skill in instructional leadership. The content presented in this book provides a starting point. Some leaders will have completed studies in high-ability and gifted education. Schools need to provide appropriate opportunities for the middle leaders to build their professional knowledge. A focus on middle leaders working as a professional learning team to build an evolving, collaborative, collective knowledge is recommended.

How will a school know when it has improved provision for high-ability and gifted students?

The unique characteristics of each school means that schools will differ in the criteria they will use to decide if improved provision has been achieved. Each leadership team can plan criteria for both students and teaching provision.

One key indicator is the portion of high-level student outcomes. A goal of the enhanced provision is that the frequency of high-level and talented outcomes and the likelihood that high-ability and gifted profiles will be converted to high-level outcomes will increase. Student voice information can provide evidence here; schools can gather data relating to the extent to which all students believe they have optimal opportunity to achieve their potential.

A second indicator is the breadth and permanence of the improved teaching practices in the work of the school. As with any area of human performance, the strategic activity in the code of teaching practice may initially be novel and would need to be practised consciously and in a piecemeal way. As it continues to be used, it will gradually become part of regular practice and be used more automatically and consistently. When it achieves the status of being part of accepted practice, it also achieves stability in the work of the school and is 'taken for granted'.

These criteria mark major points in the development of the improved provision. There is, however, a sense in which the provision will continue to develop beyond them. This is linked with ongoing changes in the context of high-ability and gifted learning.

Contemporary culture is changing in a plethora of ways; for example, in the knowledge it values and needs, in its practices, in the challenges these will generate and in the future vocations it will need. In parallel with these, conceptions of high ability and giftedness are changing, as are the opportunities contemporary culture offers to support its provision. Some of these are unpacked in Chapter 14. A school that has an enhanced provision, professional knowledge and practice for high-ability and gifted students will be better equipped to adapt to these changes.

References

Chandra Handa M (2019) 'Leading differentiated learning for the gifted', *Roeper Review*, 41(2):102–118, doi:10.1080/02783193.2019.1585213.

CHAPTER 14

Where to in future for high-ability and gifted provision?

Education practices today differ from those of 20 years ago. They are also likely to change over the next 2 decades. A school's provision for high-ability students will need to adapt to these changes. When leadership teams are aware of the likely types of changes, they will be more able to adapt to them. This chapter examines some possible future changes.

Introduction

Changes in educational provision are linked with broader changes in our world and societies. One way of describing these broader based cultural changes is in terms of megatrends; the forces that shape how we live and interact with our world (Szarkowski 4 February 2022). They include developments in technology in its multiple forms, changes in how we construct individuals and groups in a society and their freedoms, rights and responsibilities, changes in societal governance, changes in vocation and the knowledge and skills needed to participate in the future workplace, changes in how citizens communicate and interact with information and changes related to the environment, climate change and new energy sources.

These changes are likely to parallel changes in how educational provision for high ability and giftedness is conceptualised and implemented. Williams (2021) identifies 4 major influences that are expected to impact on educational provision generally: increased use of the internet, improvements in technology, distributed living and learning and a new emphasis on problem-solving and gamification. Some of these trends are already emerging in educational provision in some schools. Such changes are likely to impact on aspects of high-ability and gifted education provision in the future. They may, for example, challenge questions that have underpinned provision for decades:

> What is the IQ cut-off for being gifted?
> Is placement in a higher year the best option for every gifted student?
> How can a student who is gifted also have difficulty spelling?
> Isn't gifted education teaching, just good teaching for everyone?
> How can I teach students about a discipline when they know more about it than me?

This chapter examines current trends in high-ability and gifted provision and how these might impact on provision in the future, building on content presented in earlier chapters. Although the trends are described separately here, they are assumed to interact.

Schools that are aware of these possibilities are more likely to be 'future ready' for high-ability and gifted provision. They will be better equipped to recognise the trends and to adjust their provision to respond to them.

The main ideas in this chapter are shown in Figure 14.1.

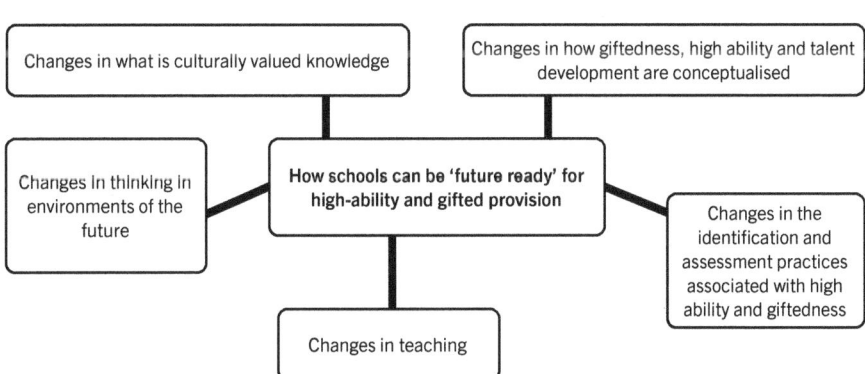

Figure 14.1. Possible changes in education practices and their impact on high-ability provision

Future trends likely to affect high-ability provision

Changes in culturally valued knowledge

Megatrends research indicates that future societal and cultural issues and challenges will require, for their resolution, knowledge that currently does not exist. Components of previously separate domains of knowledge are being integrated and traditional boundaries between subjects and domains are currently being redrawn, particularly at the tertiary level. Zurba et al. (2021:449) describe this process as interdisciplinary 'co-production'. Creativity and innovation come from linking areas of knowledge that were previously separate.

Changes in culturally valued knowledge have direct implications for curricula and how content is organised. It is likely that educational curricula in future will evolve in parallel with culturally valued knowledge. School leadership teams can tap into emerging areas of knowledge to ensure that their curriculum processes are primed to accommodate them and to ensure they have the professional knowledge required to teach in these areas and, in turn, to modify provision for high-ability students.

To move into the future, schools need to recognise high-ability learning and achievement in emerging domains. The online context offers the opportunity for providing differentiated curriculum and differentiated teaching in these domains. Future high-ability provision needs to be aware of the trends in how knowledge is evolving and of actions that might be taken to respond to these changes.

Changes in conceptualisation of high ability, giftedness and talent development

The conceptualisation of high ability and giftedness can be examined from multiple perspectives; for example, what high ability and giftedness comprises and the domains of knowledge in which it is usually displayed. A school's conceptualisation underpins the dialogue it has about high ability and giftedness and the provision it implements.

While the notion that high ability and giftedness is multifaceted has been recognised for 50 years (Marland 1971), the provision in many settings is based on the traditional models of high ability and giftedness that assume a broadly based and relatively permanent or 'fixed' high intelligence. There has been a movement away from this student-centred 'monocausal' model to one that focuses on the interaction between the student and their environment, leading to the achievement of high-level and talented outcomes (Dai 2020; Stoeger et al. 2018). This latter perspective acknowledges the opportunities the classroom culture provides for the interaction between the student and their environment. It sees a gifted learning capacity in the quality of students' responses to challenges and provocations; that is, in the intuitive theories of action they form about teaching information.

This movement from a focus on giftedness as a unitary capacity to talent development has implications for how schools talk about high ability and giftedness, the identification procedures used and the provision implemented. Rather than talking about 'gifted students', the dialogue is on the learning ability of individual students in particular domains that leads to talented or excellent outcomes (Dai 2020; Stoeger et al. 2018). It is a trend from 'how gifted is the student?' to 'how is the student gifted?'

The change in perspective can be linked with a range of trends (Stoeger et al. 2018; Papadopoulos 2021) that can broaden a school's perception of high ability and giftedness and the high-level and talented outcomes it is likely to foster as well as potentially influencing a school's future provision. Recent trends and their implications for provision include:

> the emergence of new areas of knowledge in the future and 'yet-to-exist' domains, as noted earlier. These may challenge aspects of our current conceptions of giftedness. It is recommended that schools develop their capacity to identify high-level knowledge outcomes in these areas in the future

> an increased focus on domain-specific perspectives of high ability and giftedness (VanTassel-Baska 2021). This could include the extension of provision to domains not currently included in high-ability programs, such as the Design and Technologies area of study in the Australian Curriculum and pre-vocational subjects

> a greater awareness of twice exceptionality (Amran and Majid 2019; Gierczyk and Hornby 2021) and how high learning ability can be hidden or 'masked' by a second learning exceptionality. Many twice-exceptional students, despite lack of success at school, achieve creative and talented outcomes as adults (West 2009). An implication is that schools implement procedures to cater for these students, as discussed in Chapter 5

> the recognition that cultures differ in how they conceptualise high ability and giftedness. High-ability provision in recent years has trended towards catering for students from culturally diverse backgrounds as a matter of equity. This is an appropriate focus. Chapter 5 noted how cultures differ in the way they interpret their world, the knowledge they have about it and how they think about it. A range of cultural perspectives on a topic is usually broader and richer than a single, monocultural perspective. All students can benefit from this broader exposure. With the trend towards the increasing globalisation of knowledge

and the internationalisation of education (Stromquist and Monkman 2014), schools are likely to benefit from the cultural plurality and diversity of their students.

These 4 trends can broaden a school's future understanding of what it means to be a high-ability or gifted student and the implications for provision.

New ways of thinking and emerging domains

The ways of thinking that are most useful and valued by contemporary societies are changing in parallel with the issues and challenges these societies face. The technological tools that a culture develops to respond to challenges become the ways of thinking of its members (Robbins 2005; Rogoff 2008; Säljö 2019). Historically, artefacts such as the wheel, the printing press and the light bulb resulted in significant social and cognitive developments. Examples of emerging broad-based cultural tools include artificial intelligence (Haenlein and Kaplan 2019), digital communication technology (Santos et al. 2019), machine to machine learning (Janiesch et al. 2021), big data analytics and applications (Sheng et al. 2021), and robotics (Pagliarini and Lund 2017). These phenomena, ways of thinking about them and the tools used to respond to them gradually evolve within the culture.

The potential impact of artificial intelligence to high-ability and gifted learning and its contribution to identification and teaching, discussed in Chapters 6 and 8, exemplify this. It is reasonable to expect that its increasing use will be aligned with new ways of conceptualising how individuals form, store, think about and use knowledge. This, in turn, is likely to influence how we think about gifted learning and educational provision.

High-ability students may be expected to think in advanced ways about these tools. It is possible that students may require new forms of metacognition, self-agency, independence and entrepreneurial thinking to do this. The thinking and actions needed to generate high-level outcomes in the emerging areas of knowledge will need to be supported by the learning contexts. Schools may need to decide the characteristics of learning environments of the future that will be needed to support the high-ability thinking.

Contemporary models of talent development stress the importance of the quality of the interactions scaffolded by the context; in this case, the classroom. Changes in thinking and actions for high-level outcomes accordingly need to be scaffolded by appropriate learning contexts. These learning contexts also need the appropriate environmental characteristics to support transformational thinking in emerging domains.

In summary, high-ability and gifted provision in the future will need to recognise and take account of the emergence of different ways of thinking and the characteristics of contexts needed to support them.

Changes in identification and assessment associated with high ability and giftedness

With the continuing development of online assessment platforms and more powerful analytics engines, information collection and interpretation are likely to improve the identification process associated with high ability and giftedness. This includes:

> collecting, interpreting and analysing outcome and learning data over the course of learning activities, rather than one-off assessments

> personalising the tasks used and the conditions under which individual students engage with and respond to them

> identifying the domains and contexts in which individual students display high-level outcomes

> tracking students' learning progress to identify the conditions when high-level outcomes are displayed

> interpreting and evaluating the assessment information rapidly and efficiently, permitting efficient decision-making.

Some of the current trends in online assessment of high-ability learning profiles and high-level outcomes were noted in Chapter 7. Two trends likely to influence identification in the future are changes in what is assessed and how the assessment is implemented.

In terms of what is assessed for identification, there is a trend away from general ability or intelligence testing to the identification of high-level or talented outcomes in specific disciplines, often in response to provocations and problems (Dai 2020; Sternberg 2022). Identification is likely to indicate the domains, disciplines or aspects of the curriculum in which an individual has high ability and giftedness.

There is also a trend in the types of assessment tasks that will be used (Dai 2020; Sternberg 2022). Future assessment protocols may preference assessing the quality of students' knowledge in open-ended productions, such as authentic projects, performance tasks, complex problem-solving and responses to provocations rather than to traditional test items. This type of assessment could arguably extend current general ability assessments and present a more comprehensive evaluation of a student's potential and capacity to form intuitive theories of action.

General ability assessments will probably continue to have a role, but not to compare students' overall intellectual ability. Chapter 7 describes how these assessments can be used to infer the characteristics of a high-ability student's learning profile once a student has been identified as displaying excellent outcomes in a domain. The focus is on comparing the student's reasoning ability in several areas, rather than their overall outcomes with norms.

One aspect of this trend is a move from a focus on the interpretation of normative data to a focus on personalisation of learning. Dai (2020:1523) describes this aspect as follows: 'giftedness is not based on some arbitrary cut-offs of psychometrically defined individual differences, but distinct ways the person interacts with his or her task and social environments'. The identification procedures described in Chapters 6 and 7 reflect this trend.

In terms of how high-ability identification is implemented generally, there is a trend away from traditional standardised testing frameworks to digital assessments that use adaptive procedures. These allow educators to identify a student's knowledge and ways of thinking regardless of their year or age level.

Rather than using identification practices that use one-point-in-time assessment scores, emerging technology will allow educators to collect multiple types of student data at various times across a student's education trajectory. Examples of this technology are provided by

Gustafsson-Wright et al. (2022) and include apps, online assessments, data analysis software and machine learning. This technology also has the potential to interpret the data rapidly and identify high-ability and gifted learning profiles and talented outcomes across a range of domains.

It is likely that procedures that convert assessment data to digital forms will be able to employ multiple formats for assessing students' outcomes (Paleczek et al. 2021). This will probably include assessments of performance 'in the field' (Henny 1 June 2016); for example, while students are pursuing investigations and research projects, applying their knowledge, problem-solving or generating open-ended outcomes. These can include identifying the conditions under which talented outcomes are optimised for an individual student, possibly drawing on the set of dynamic assessment procedures described in Chapter 7. This could provide increased equity for the multiple high-ability profiles to display their potential and could take account of twice-exceptional profiles. These procedures also allow educators to track student performance and measure learning improvement over time.

One aspect of the increased focus on personalising identification of high ability has involved a movement to taking account of the contexts in which the high-level outcomes are displayed. This includes interpreting a student's outcomes in terms of their learning and developmental history. It also includes using local rather than national norms to interpret student data; the local norms take account of local environmental conditions (Lohman 2009).

In summary, future identification protocols are likely to monitor how students respond to various teaching and contextual conditions in increasingly dynamic and automated ways and may result in teachers' increased ability to identify high ability and giftedness in students.

Changes in teaching and learning

Societal changes and developments in digital technologies offer the opportunity for providing curriculum teaching and learning cultures that are differentiated to match individual high-ability learning profiles as well as the opportunity for learning collaboratively with 'like-minded' peers and for enhancing social-interactional skills.

The capacity to personalise provision is matched by a change in the thinking that underpins the provision. This is a shift from a focus on high-ability and gifted students as homogenous groups or categories, to a focus on the learning capacities and profiles of individual students who achieve high-level and excellent outcomes. This change has implications for how high ability and giftedness are constructed for educational provision.

Emerging technologies, such as augmented reality, virtual reality and machine learning, can be embedded in discipline knowledge to facilitate opportunities for individualised learning, both collaboratively and with the many online information sources relevant to topics students are learning that are likely to increase in breadth and depth. These technologies can also provide teaching information and learning contexts that scaffold students' generation of their intuitive theories of action and that can be particularly important for students with non-verbal and performance learning profiles.

E-learning will lead to improved provision for the personalised learning of high-ability and gifted students by providing teachers with tools to monitor transitory changes in students' knowledge in a domain, how they think about the domain and their learning profile. It offers an enhanced capacity to monitor changes in the understanding of individual students during learning and to adjust teaching formatively to match how they are progressing at that time (Jethro et al. 2012; Samsuri et al. 2014; Wang 2014). In this way, high-ability students will have enhanced access to differentiated teaching that adjusts to and aligns with how they learn. The provision can adjust to the multiple high-ability profiles and take account of twice-exceptional profiles. This permits learning pathways to an outcome that take account of individual learning profiles.

Teachers will be more able to monitor, direct and scaffold student learning activity. E-learning offers students the opportunity to pursue knowledge in an open-ended way, to be curious and to manage and direct aspects of their learning activity. Students will be more able to engage in self-paced and self-managed learning, at different times and in different places. They will have greater opportunity to select their preferred programs, to engage in blended learning and flipped classrooms and to have personalised mentoring.

Contexts used for teaching and learning include physical environments enriched with computer-generated visual and sound information (augmented reality) and computer-generated simulated environments (virtual reality). Technology is beginning to stimulate various senses, including touch, motion and feelings.

Opportunities for acceleration are also likely to be enhanced. Opportunities for subject- and year-based differentiation are likely to be improved through online provision. These provisions are more likely to match the multidimensional aspects of a student's learning profile (such as their cognitive ability and social interaction skills). High-ability students will be more able to access appropriate high-level teaching and differentiated curriculum while remaining in a peer-group cohort that matches their social interactional, emotional and physical abilities. This can also mean that year-level acceleration may be less necessary in some situations.

Virtual classrooms and Massive Open Online Courses (MOOCs) provide opportunities for high-ability students to access differentiated curricula and to engage in collaborative interactive learning with like-minded peers. Distributed learning systems (Chen et al. 2021) allow teachers, students and content to be in different locations and offer access to teaching that is independent of time and place. They provide the opportunity for students to share and synthesise their intuitive theories of action about complex problems and to infer solutions. These environments provide the opportunity for high-ability and gifted students to model and simulate reality, trial the possibilities in their intuitive theories of action and engage in complex problem-solving.

Gamification is another emerging instructional approach that teaches in a game-like context and that embodies the notion of learning by responding to provocations or challenges. This approach is particularly appropriate for high-ability and gifted students. It provides challenges and facilitates student thinking and activity, leading to new knowledge as students play. The types and amount of information in a game context, the topic or theme of a game, the types of thinking required to play the game, the sequence and timing of actions in the game and the complexity of the metacognition needed to participate can all be matched to aspects of students' existing knowledge.

Online learning programs in future may also be better equipped to respond to situations in which, as has been discussed earlier in this book, some high-ability and gifted students display emotional and social issues in the classroom (Plucker and Callahan 2014). Where this occurs, it is often associated with the beliefs formed by high-ability students about how their knowledge and thinking differs from that of their same-age peers and the extent to which it is valued by the classroom culture. Online programs offer the possibility of more systematic and effective feedback schedules for what these students know. They can also provide opportunities for these students to share their knowledge and thinking in online contexts with high-ability and regular students in collaborative activities. The online collaborative activities can assist with improving social skills and emotional management in non-threatening contexts.

Stepping into the future

Future trends will be paralleled by a change in the role of educators. With ready access to appropriate curriculum, information sources and learning activities, teachers of high-ability students will probably take a more learning–mentoring approach, acting as 'coaches of high ability'. This will include teaching a broad range of learning and knowledge-enhancement strategies, research and information literacy skills. Teachers will still have the roles of encouraging students' curiosity and interest, of guiding their learning activity and of supporting their emotional and social wellbeing. They will also need a functional understanding of the emerging technology and their role in it as learning mentors.

More generally, school structures will need to adjust to accommodate trends. Leaders will need to direct the school-level shifts to permit the changes described above. Schools in the future may explore how emerging technology can help them to form partnerships with community institutions to broaden the range of learning opportunities. These could include linking topics in the curriculum with community issues and innovations. Virtual and augmented reality, for example, can provide students with access to instances of issues that challenge their community, for example, in health, transport, energy generation, employment or climate change. These technologies allow students to explore and problem-solve these types of issues in simulated contexts; they effectively bring community issues into the classroom. These activities provide the opportunity for high-ability and gifted students to experience how their advanced knowledge can be applied to respond to contemporary challenges in their world.

Developments such as those involving new cultural values, technology and emerging domains, changes in online assessment and learning and new conceptualisation of high-ability and giftedness offer exciting opportunities for all students. Schools will be more able to adapt to them in a self-directing way when they have developed the professional knowledge and provision described in this book. Your school can begin the move into the future now.

Summary

Societal trends in the future are likely to lead to matching changes in high-ability provision.

How can schools be 'future ready' for changes in:

- what is culturally valued knowledge
- how giftedness and high ability and talent development are conceptualised
- thinking in environments of the future
- the personalisation of learning
- the identification and assessment practices associated with high ability and giftedness
- teaching provision?

School structures will need to change to accommodate these trends. The professional knowledge and provision described in Chapters 1 to 12 provides a foundation for accommodating these changes.

References

Amran HA and Majid RA (2019) 'Learning strategies for twice-exceptional students', *International Journal of Special Education*, 33(4):954–976.

Chen M, Gündüz D, Huang K, Saad W, Bennis M, Feljan AV and Poor HV (2021) 'Distributed learning in wireless networks: recent progress and future challenges', *IEEE Journal on Selected Areas in Communications*, 39(12):3579–3605, doi:10.1109/JSAC.2021.3118346.

Dai DY (2020) 'Assessing and accessing high human potential: a brief history of giftedness and what it means to school psychologists', *Psychology in the Schools*, 57(10):1514–1527, doi:10.1002/pits.22346.

Gierczyk M and Hornby G (2021) 'Twice-exceptional students: review of implications for special and inclusive education', *Education Sciences*, 11(2):85–94, doi:10.3390/educsci11020085.

Gustafsson-Wright E, Osborne S and Aggarwal M (2022) *Digital tools for real-time data collection in education*, Brookings Institution, accessed 14 March 2024. https://policycommons.net/artifacts/4142237/digital-tools-for-real-time-data-collection-in-education/4951284/

Haenlein M and Kaplan A (2019) 'A brief history of artificial intelligence: on the past, present, and future of artificial intelligence', *California Management Review*, 61(4):5–14, doi:10.1177/00081256198649.

Henny C (1 June 2016) '9 things that will shape the future of education: what learning will look like in 20 years?', *eLearning Trends*, eLearning Industry, Reno, NV, accessed 2 November 2023. https://elearningindustry.com/9-things-shape-future-of-education-learning-20-years

Janiesch C, Zschech P and Heinrich K (2021) 'Machine learning and deep learning', *Electronic Markets*, 31(3):685-695, doi:10.1007/s12525-021-00475-2.

Jethro OO, Grace AM and Thomas AK (2012) 'E-learning and its effects on teaching and learning in a global age', *International Journal of Academic Research in Business and Social Sciences*, 2(1):203–210.

Lohman DF (2009) 'Identifying academically talented students: some general principles, two specific procedures', in Shavinina LV (ed) *International handbook on giftedness*, Springer, Dordrecht, doi:10.1007/978-1-4020-6162-2.

Marland Jr SP (1971) *Education of the gifted and talented-volume 1: report to the Congress of the United States by the US Commissioner of Education*, Department of Education, Department of Health, Education, and Welfare, Washington, DC.

Pagliarini L and Lund HH (2017) 'The future of robotics technology', *Journal of Robotics, Networking and Artificial Life*, 3(4):270–273.

Paleczek L, Seifert S and Schöfl M (2021) 'Comparing digital to print assessment of receptive vocabulary with GraWo-KiGa in Austrian kindergarten', *British Journal of Educational Technology*, 52(6):2145–2161, doi:10.1111/bjet.13163.

Papadopoulos D (2021) 'Examining the relationships among cognitive ability, domain-specific self-concept, and behavioral self-esteem of gifted children aged 5–6 years: a cross-sectional study', *Behavioral Sciences*, 11(7):93, doi:10.3390/bs11070093.

Plucker JA and Callahan CM (2014) 'Research on giftedness and gifted education: status of the field and considerations for the future', *Exceptional Children*, 80(4):390–406, doi:10.1177/0014402914527244.

Robbins J (2005) 'Contexts, collaboration, and cultural tools: a sociocultural perspective on researching children's thinking', *Contemporary Issues in Early Childhood*, 6(2):140–149.

Rogoff B (2008) 'Thinking with the tools and institutions of culture', in Murphy P and Hall K (eds) *Learning and practice: agency and identities*, SAGE Publications, London.

Säljö R (2019) 'Materiality, learning, and cognitive practices: artifacts as instruments of thinking', in Pargman TC and Jahnke I (eds) *Emergent practices and material conditions in learning and teaching with technologies*, Springer Nature, Cham, Switzerland.

Samsuri NN, Nadzri FA and Rom KBM (2014) 'A study on the student's perspective on the effectiveness of using e-learning', *Procedia-Social and Behavioral Sciences*, 123:139–144, doi:10.1016/j.sbspro.2014.01.1407.

Santos H, Batista J and Marques RP (2019) 'Digital transformation in higher education: the use of communication technologies by students', *Procedia Computer Science*, 164:123–130, doi:10.1016/j.procs.2019.12.163.

Sheng J, Amankwah-Amoah J, Khan Z and Wang X (2021) 'COVID-19 pandemic in the new era of big data analytics: methodological innovations and future research directions', *British Journal of Management*, 32(4):1164–1183, doi:10.1111/1467-8551.12441.

Sternberg RJ (2022) 'Transformational giftedness: who's got it and who does not', in *The Palgrave handbook of transformational giftedness for education*, Springer International Publishing, Cham, Switzerland.

Stoeger H, Balestrini DP and Ziegler A (2018) 'International perspectives and trends in research on giftedness and talent development', in Pfeiffer SI, Shaunessy-Dedrick E and Foley-Nicpon M (eds) *APA handbook of giftedness and talent*, American Psychological Association, Washington DC.

Stromquist NP and Monkman K (2014) 'Defining globalization and assessing its implications for knowledge and education, revisited', in Stromquist NP and Monkman K (eds) *Globalization and education: integration and contestation across cultures*, 2nd edn, Rowman & Littlefield Education, Lanham, MD.

Szarkowski S (4 February 2022) 'What in the world (in 2050) is a megatrend?', *Diplomatic Courier*, Washington, DC, accessed 2 November 2023. https://www.diplomaticourier.com/posts/what-in-the-world-in-2050-is-a-megatrend

VanTassel-Baska J (2021) 'A conception of giftedness as domain-specific learning: a dynamism fueled by persistence and passion', in Sternberg RJ and Ambrose D (eds) *Conceptions of giftedness and talent*, Palgrave Macmillan, Cham, Switzerland.

Wang TH (2014) 'Developing an assessment-centered e-Learning system for improving student learning effectiveness', *Computers & Education*, 73:189-203, doi:10.1016/j.compedu.2013.12.002.

West TG (2013) *In the mind's eye: visual thinkers, gifted people with learning difficulties, computer images, and the ironies of creativity*, Prometheus Books, Buffalo, New York.

Zurba M, Petriello MA, Madge C, McCarney P, Bishop B, McBeth S, Denniston M, Bodwitch H and Bailey M (2021) 'Learning from knowledge co-production research and practice in the twenty-first century: global lessons and what they mean for collaborative research in Nunatsiavut', *Sustainability Science*, 17:449–467, doi:10.1007/s11625-021-00996.

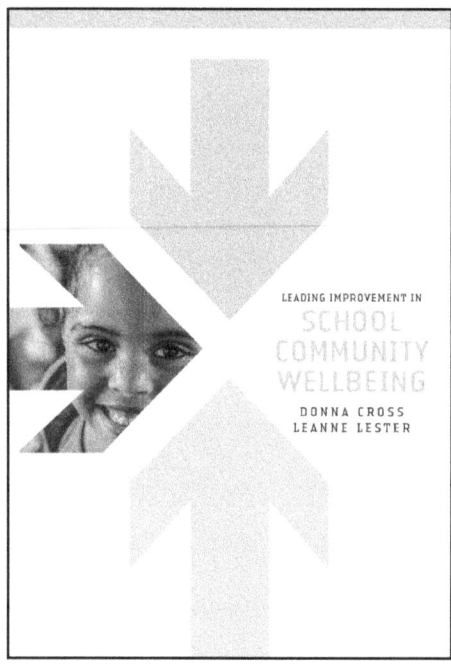

EXTEND YOUR IMPACT WITH FURTHER TITLES FROM THE

'HIGH IMPACT STRATEGIES FOR SCHOOL LEADERS' SERIES.

www.ambapress.com.au

www.ingramcontent.com/pod-product-compliance
Lightning Source LLC
Chambersburg PA
CBHW061123070526
44584CB00033B/4208